100WORDS

200 **Visionaries**

Share Their Hope for the Future

William Murtha

Conari
Press

First published in 2010 by Conari Press,
an imprint of Red Wheel/Weiser, LLC
With offices at:
500 Third Street, Suite 230
San Francisco, CA 94107
www.redwheelweiser.com

ISBN: 978-1-57324-473-2
Library of Congress Cataloging-in-Publication Data available upon request.

Cover and text design by Stewart A. Williams
Typeset in Helvetica Neue
Cover photograph © Daniel Talbott

Printed in Canada
TCP
10 9 8 7 6 5 4 3 2 1

❀ Printed on 100% recycled paper.

Gratitude

Warm and sincere thanks to the motivators and visionaries, the leaders and social changers, who have all contributed to this astonishing project. You have each walked your talk, and in doing so, inspired countless others to be the change.

Thank you all for donating your vision statements to this worldwide project, and know that many more inspirational writers and filmmakers will now benefit from your kind actions.

Very best wishes to my publisher, Jan Johnson, and the whole team at Red Wheel. You have all contributed immensely in helping to make *100 Words* the success it is today.

To Jayne, I thank you for your unwavering belief in this amazing project. At times when I have come so precariously close to the brink, you have always been there to pull me back, with your unconditional love, support, and guidance.

And to my dear friend and writing mentor, Katy Clarke. The first person in the world to hear out my plan for the whole Global Visionaries Project. Your positive early feedback was essential in helping this book to take its first breath on what was unquestionably the road less traveled.

What the World Needs Now

One thing the world needs now is people who can tolerate ambiguity, people who are challenged, not threatened by the state of the world. I want to suggest a few things such maturity might require. . . .

First, do not seek security in things, nor yet in status. The care of possessions, and position, is time-consuming and energy-consuming, and they can be taken from you by a thief in the night, by a fire in the night, by a change of political fortunes, by any number of disasters. Whatever security you have lies in yourself. Henceforth I ask not good fortune. I myself am good fortune.

If you understand yourself, both your strengths and limitations, if you like the person you are, if you acquire coping skills through experience, if you are not too encumbered, and if you know—inwardly—that disaster cannot ultimately overcome you, then you have gone a long way to maturity. You will be part of the solution, not part of the problem.

Second, don't rest in intellectual security, for your philosophy and the knowledge on which it rests are likely to become obsolete. Wisdom is not amassing facts.

Third, the only real security in the end is the love we have given and the love we have received. All else can be taken from us. So pour out your love and friendship and do not hoard it. And don't delay or hesitate in standing up to be counted with the oppressed.

Finally, cultivate the light touch. Develop a sense of humour. Learn to light up a room with joy when you enter. Accept the challenge of our chaotic and dangerous world with a sense of adventure, of gratitude that our time is now.

Elizabeth Watson
peace activist and humanitarian, 1838–1919

Introduction

"The greatest danger to our future is apathy."
—Jane Goodall

Few would argue that a new world order is emerging out of the chaos of the past several decades.

As we rapidly accelerate away from that outdated model of capitalism and wealth creation that my baby-boomer generation was expected to embrace, we witness the blossoming of a new way of living and connecting in the world. Age-old institutions and financial systems are disintegrating, and as we watch unworkable ideologies crumble to dust, there is much cause for celebration amongst the darkness and despair:

We are a race awakening to its highest potential.

Don't get me wrong, this global transformation of consciousness, like most new births, is excruciatingly painful, and it certainly won't be plain sailing. But rising from the ashes of this previously unjust and unsustainable economic model is hopefully going to evolve a more enlightened, empathic, peaceful, connected, and consciously aware society. After the traumatic and sometimes disturbing economic events of the past few years, it's now becoming crystal clear to an increasing number of people that a global shakedown was absolutely essential. It's become evermore apparent that *we* needed to change to ensure that all life can continue to go on.

As the planet's population rapidly edges ever closer to seven billion (far more than its natural carrying capacity), more and more of us are waking up to the reality that an inner transformation in our thinking and attitudes had to occur. We simply couldn't maintain those self-destructive habits that were poisoning our planet, our bodies, and our minds. What's become more apparent to us during these times of obsessive greed and material wealth, of affluence beyond measure and so-called abundance, is that something vital was missing from our lives. We'd become so disconnected not only from other people and the very environment that sustains us, but also disconnected from our true values. The constant and ever-growing sense of pervading restlessness, which is now so visibly endemic throughout modern society, is today being fully recognized as a cry from the collective soul for change. We are slowly waking up to see that life can't carry on this way forever.

Life *had* to change. *We* had to change.

Many are coming to the conclusion that the ways in which we lived and worked yesterday won't necessarily work today. And we're also realizing that it's impossible to continue living in a manner that's deeply destructive to the Earth's ecosystem—the very biosphere and life-support that shelters, feeds, and nourishes our bodies, minds, and souls. But most of all, it's starting to hit home that we cannot continue plundering the Earth's limited resources when we only have a finite planet. The math simply doesn't add up. Sooner or later, something, or rather someone (usually being the poorest and less able amongst us), will suffer.

For the past four years, I have been fortunate enough to meet up with, speak to, and connect with many of the world's most prominent visionaries and luminaries of our time, change-makers and leaders who are pioneers in this global transformation that we are now witnessing. My travels and meetings have allowed me to appreciate many of the planet's most critically important issues that we now face, including climate change, environmental degradation, and social injustice. I've met many of those inspired teachers who, through dogged determination and sheer will, are literally changing the world from the inside out. These are the passionate activists and way-showers, the doers on the ground who have been gifted with the insight and vision to imagine new and more expanded possibilities for an ever-awakening human race.

This book, *100 Words: 200 Visionaries Share Their Hope for the Future,* is a testament to their hopes, resilience, courage, and life-message. This is their story. And best of all, their uplifting and sometimes courageous stories clearly demonstrate much of what is going right in the world. While pulling together this wide range of positive vision statements, what soon became apparent to me is the amount of sacrifice that had to be made, as those visionaries represented here fought to keep hold of their dreams and visions for a better future. Taking the road less traveled for those daring to challenge the status quo was far from easy and often involved a great deal of pain, retribution, and self-sacrifice. As many of us have experienced, it's not easy to swim against the rushing torrent of a capitalist ideal—one that constantly preaches a God of continuous growth and increasing profits. It can be exhausting and painful when we dare to challenge the existing dogma. Far easier is it to put up and shut up, to go with the flow and live a more quiet and mundane existence.

That may well be true for the majority who simply accept that the world will never change. But it is certainly not true for all the visionaries featured here. These paradigm-shifters and innovators—dedicated to developing new ways of living and being in the world—are conscious that their ideas are often not welcome. They know that they will bump up against destructive ideologies that have little or no desire for change—systems of authority and corporate governance that do not want their comfortable ways either questioned or challenged.

You see, there is a small minority in the world which has too much self-interest and investment in society remaining stuck where it is. These people do not invite in the promise of transformation, self-realization, or social change because it doesn't suit their cause. Worse still, it certainly doesn't feed their balance sheets, profits, or power base. These power brokers, government leaders, and corporate heads have prospered under a controlling globalized system of trade barriers and protectionism, one that delivers increasing wealth and abundance to only the select few, even though this guarantees that billions of others less fortunate remain chained to poverty.

The enlightening news is that this ideology is coming off the rails, disintegrating before our very eyes. Why? Because greater numbers of people are fast realizing that this outdated and grossly unjust economic model, which cares little for people's well-being or the planet, does not serve those nations or individuals at the bottom of the pile. Whatever shocking and depressing statistics you care to look at, they all point to the same truth: our present system of economics simply doesn't work anymore.

What's equally frightening in today's changing world is that even the previously untouchable and impregnable middle class of the West—the engine house of previous economic miracles—is now also becoming vulnerable and financially exposed to this growing sense of hopelessness and desperation.

They too are being sucked into different forms of poverty, be it dietary, mental, social, or financial. Whatever region of the world we look at, it's abundantly clear that increasing numbers of global citizens are feeling a collective sense of disquiet, detachment, and confusion. Combine this with the growing rage, anger, and anxiety that is welling up against this system that no longer works, and we truly have a perfect storm brewing for increasing dysfunction throughout modern society.

So if our twenty-first-century way of living is veering radically off course, what's happening to change it? Who are the motivators behind inspiring new and better ways of living? What positive impact can their grassroots work have on an everyday, grounded level? What new initiatives and projects are addressing these problems of inequality and social injustice? And what radical differences can we expect to see in the decade ahead, as this citizen movement for change starts to pick up pace?

Read on and you'll be inspired by what you discover. Because contrary to much of the violence and negativity that we are fed on the six o'clock news, there are still countless stories of hope and community punching through to lift our spirits. What you'll discover after reading this positive commentary is that there is an unnamed movement for change building around the world. This movement may fly under the radar of the core media, but nevertheless, it is a growing movement of everyday people who believe that their collective actions really can inspire a better tomorrow. These are everyday people like you and me who are passionately committed to creating more sustainable and life-fulfilling ways of living and connecting in the world.

The uplifting and empowering words delivered from these visionaries will, I hope, inspire you to also become a change-maker and activist for transformation. Their insights and experiences will inject you with an unshakable belief that you too can become a leading light in the world. Let's hope so. Let's hope that reading these golden nuggets of collective wisdom really can fire up something from deep within your heart and soul. Perhaps these encouraging messages of hope—not to mention the incredible human stories behind them—really do possess the stimulus to inspire us all to embrace our highest potential, and therefore activate our own calling and purpose in life.

As I've mentioned already, a new and more awakened planet is emerging out of this economic and social chaos that we are painfully observing every day. A new world order is being born out of the personal crises that can so often threaten to overwhelm and paralyze us. But let's look beyond those darker and more painful moments and see that, on the horizon, something far more beautiful and life-sustaining is being called forward.

The vision statements that have been contributed to this unique initiative, *100 Words,* clearly demonstrate that we are never alone in how we feel. These profound messages clearly show that we are never isolated from the collective pain we tune in to when witnessing disturbing images of social chaos or environmental breakdown. As most of the world's most renowned spiritual pioneers have taught us, we really are one: together in both our joy and our pain. Just know that more innovators and visionaries than you'd ever imagine not only feel the same way as you and I do, they are also working tirelessly to engineer a safer and more life-sustaining way of being.

When you come to realize that this movement for change is not only taking, but building up incredible momentum, it will make your heart sing. I know mine did when I started to realize that this growing band of change-makers is to be found in every corner of life. What struck me even more was that this global movement was on an unprecedented scale. Nothing like this has ever happened before. Never in history have so many people felt compelled and driven to act against political disease, social injustice, and environmental destruction. What we are witnessing during our lifetimes (and Paul Hawken, the American activist and environmentalist, eloquently expressed this in his book, *Blessed Unrest*) is "humanity's immune response" to resist that which we know to be deeply unethical.

We are truly blessed to be alive at this most critical juncture in history, a time when our collective efforts really can contribute the kind of world that our children and future generations deserve to inherit. With the passion and desire, the intention and the belief, we really can be visionaries and change agents. We can all contribute by answering that calling deep within, which begs us to sit up, pay attention, and listen to our hearts. What *100 Words* is showing us through the activism of others is that individually we can all make small, meaningful differences.

But together we truly can transform the world.

The inspirational change-makers featured in this book may be only a tiny representation of those who are daring to dream of a better world. They may well be only droplets in the ocean of much-needed change. But, as Mother Teresa profoundly commented, "The ocean is made up of drops."

William L. Murtha
Devon, England, UK, August 2009

The Inspiration Behind the Book

During the past four years while travelling around the world as a speaker and writer, I have been astonished at the breadth and depth of new initiatives that are springing up everywhere. Inspirational and positive causes that are passionately evolving, in response to the growing human desire we all have to find better meaning and purpose in our lives. I've also been pleasantly surprised at the sheer size of this combined force of global activists and visionaries—being that their much valued work is seldom reported in the mainstream media, a sometimes biased media that, by and large, seem constantly fixated on everything that's failing in the world. However, fueled by hope, I kept on digging and probing, and to my astonishment, I quickly discovered a thriving movement of nongovernmental organizations and social innovators who were literally healing and changing the world—one project at a time.

Totally inspired by some of the positive stories I'd unearthed, I created *100 Words,* an initiative that would focus on everything that was going right in the world. I wanted to show some of the many inspirational projects that were evolving out of a human need to bring more balance and connection into the world. And most of all, my desire was to get a glimpse of the innovators who are driving these changes forward, changes that are essential to our search for a more hopeful, meaningful, and healthy future.

Full of hope, and inspired by all of the incredible human stories I encountered, I sent out invitations to over five hundred of these dedicated luminaries and change-makers, all of them at the forefront of global transformation in their specialized fields.

My request to each of them was the same:

Given the enormity of problems now facing planet Earth at this critical juncture, please let me have your positive vision and hopes for the future.

Put another way, in around 100 words, please share empowering stories and thoughts that can best encapsulate your insight, wisdom, and feelings on how we can move toward a more just, fulfilling, and peaceful world.

I followed this by asking each:

What five books, poems or songs have most inspired both your life and your vocation? (As you will see, some chose not to provide a list.)

This book documents what these extraordinary inspirers had to say. . . .

THE VISION
STATEMENTS

Who Is Kathleen Adams?

Kathleen Adams, founder and director of the Center for Journal Therapy in Denver, is one of the leading teachers and theorists in the field of therapeutic writing. She teaches a graduate program in Writing & Healing at the University of Denver and is on the faculty of Cross Country Education, teaching journal therapy to psychotherapists. She is the author of six books on journal writing, including the bestselling *Journal to the Self* (Warner Books). She has several training programs that prepare individuals to facilitate journal groups in their own communities. www.journaltherapy.com

THREE BOOKS, ONE POEM, AND A WORKSHOP THAT HAVE CHANGED KATHLEEN'S LIFE:

Pilgrim at Tinker Creek, Annie Dillard

The New Diary, Tristine Rainer

The Transformers, Jacquelyn Small

"Renascence," Edna St. Vincent Millay

The Intensive Journal® workshop, created by Dr. Ira Progoff

KATHLEEN
ADAMS

My passion is making the healing art of journal writing accessible to all who desire self-directed change. We're getting close to the "tipping point"—the common acknowledgment that writing down thoughts and feelings in a way that supports insight and growth helps people feel more settled, clear, and peaceful. Since people who are at peace within themselves tend to seek peaceful resolutions to conflict, journal writing is a powerful change agent in the world. My lifetime vision is to contribute to lasting peace on our troubled planet. My instruments of change are journals—along with my voice and my advocacy in helping people write their own ways to personal peace and freedom.

Who Is Carol Adrienne?

Carol Adrienne, PhD, an intuitive life coach, is also an internationally known workshop facilitator and author whose books have been translated into over fifteen languages. Her books include *The Purpose of Your Life* (as seen on *Oprah*); *Find Your Purpose, Change Your Life;* and *When Life Changes or You Wish It Would*. She is also coauthor with James Redfield of *The Celestine Prophecy: An Experiential Guide*. Her first book, *The Numerology Kit*, was published in 1988; she followed it up with *Your Child's Destiny*. In 2007 three new books on numerology and life skills were published in Japanese. Carol is based in El Cerrito, California. www.caroladrienne.com

BOOKS THAT HAVE INFLUENCED CAROL'S LIFE:
How Proust Can Change Your Life, Alain de Botton
Exploring Reincarnation, Hans TenDam
Numerology, Dr. Juno Jordan
The Celestine Prophecy, James Redfield
If You Want to Write, Brenda Ueland

CAROL
ADRIENNE

When beginning a thing, I think you have to make sure that your motivation is pure (that you really want to do this thing or there is a very good practical reason to do this thing, and that it's not going to be harmful to anyone else). In the middle of a thing, if it's still worth doing (like being a parent), keep working through the obstacles (or wait them out). The trick is learning the difference between when to persevere and when to let go. At the end of a thing, it's important to be grateful for what you gained or learned, but don't keep going back there. Stay in the present.

Who Is Julian Agyeman?

Julian is associate professor and chair of the Department of Urban and Environmental Policy and Planning at Tufts University, Boston-Medford. He is coeditor of the journal *Local Environment: The International Journal of Justice and Sustainability*. His books include *Local Environmental Policies and Strategies*, *Just Sustainabilities: Development in an Unequal World*, *Sustainable Communities and the Challenge of Environmental Justice*, and *The New Countryside? Ethnicity, Nation and Exclusion in Contemporary Rural Britain*. Julian is a Fellow of the Royal Society of Arts (FRSA), is a member of the board of directors of the Center for Whole Communities in Vermont, and is on numerous editorial boards.

BOOKS AND SONGS THAT HAVE INSPIRED JULIAN:
Small Is Beautiful, E. F. Schumacher
Zen and the Art of Motorcycle Maintenance, Robert Pirsig
"Song of the Wind," Santana
"Parce Mihi Domine," Jan Garbarek and the Hilliard Ensemble
"Light My Fire," The Doors

JULIAN
AGYEMAN

Sustainable development means using *our unlimited mental resources*, not our *limited natural resources*. If this is true, as I believe it to be, then we need to develop constructive ways to unleash these phenomenal mental resources, and quickly. Currently, we waste human potential as wantonly and comprehensively as we lay waste to our environmental potential, and this is no surprise, as both actions are directly related. We need to mobilize our efforts toward developing the potential of *all* humans *in order to* live productively in a convivial manner within environmental limits. Failure to do so will end our ability to approach anything near the just and sustainable futures we are capable of.

Who Is Paul Allen?

Paul is currently the development director at the Centre for Alternative Technology (CAT) in the United Kingdom. His current projects include the £6.2 million Wales Institute for Sustainable Education—a unique learning environment in which students and professionals can meet to discover a range of sustainable solutions, and an environment that will also embody and demonstrate these same sustainability principles in working practice. Paul was the project director of the ground-breaking energy strategy ZeroCarbonBritain and the author of a wide range of publications and feature articles on the issues related to sustainable technologies and lifestyles. Before working at CAT, Paul was a director of Dulas Engineering Ltd, where he was responsible for the design, development, and production of a wide variety of renewable energy projects, including solar-powered vaccine refrigeration as well as hospital and emergency systems. www.cat.org.uk

FIVE OF PAUL'S FAVORITE BOOKS:

Powerdown, Richard Heinberg
Heat, George Monbiot
The Hidden Persuaders, Vance Packard
The Turning Point, Fritjof Capra
The Field, Lynne McTaggart

PAUL
ALLEN

We must urgently face our addiction to fossil fuels and embark on a transition to zero carbon emissions quickly. This is at the very boundaries of what is "politically thinkable," and is a challenge for our society, democracy, and our technology. ZeroCarbonBritain offers a means of integrating our knowledge and experience into a coherent vision that can be effectively articulated to endorse local action and to inform our elected representatives. A "zero carbon transition" is scientifically urgent, economically inescapable, and technically possible. And it will entail a challenging period in our history, requiring bold decision-making and an urgent sense of common purpose. Life as it is will change, like it or not. But if we act now, with confidence, rising to this challenge will mean ingenuity replaces apathy, and self-reliance replaces self-gratification, and it just might deliver a rich sense of collective purpose and individual meaning, which we find we have been craving for a very long time.

Who Is Dr. A. T. Ariyaratne?

Ahangamage Tudor Ariyaratne was born November 5, 1931, in Sri Lanka. He had four sisters and a brother. His father was a businessman. They were a very devout Buddhist family. He studied first in the village school, then at Mahinda College, Galle, and the Vidyodaya University of Sri Lanka. He started the Sarvodaya Shramadana Movement of Sri Lanka in 1958 and pioneered the people's movement that over the last fifty years has developed into a mass movement for the total regeneration of Sri Lanka, where it is active in fifteen thousand villages. For his innovative work in humanitarian services and peace, he was awarded in 1969 the Ramon Magsaysay Award for Community Leadership, and in 1982 the King Baudouin Award for International Development from Belgium. In 1992 he received the Mahatma Gandhi Peace Award and, to date, countless other international and national awards. In 2007 the president of Sri Lanka decorated him with the country's highest honor, the Deshabhimani (Pride of Sri Lanka) Award.

WORKS THAT HAVE IMPRESSED A. T. ARIYARATNE:

Life of the Buddha, Ven. Ananda Maitreya Thero
A Manual of Buddhism, Ven. Narada Thero
An Autobiography, Mahatma Gandhi
Autobiography of a Yogi, Paramahansa Yogananda
Shakespeare's plays

DR. A. T.
ARIYARATNE

I can transcend my "ego," my "self," if I consciously breathe in universal energies and feel I am a part of the universe and the universe is part of me. This feeling gives rise to a new relationship between myself, my society, and my environment. This relationship is based on unconditional love for all living beings. Race, class, color, political ideologies, and creed can no longer separate us. Loving kindness, compassionate actions, altruistic joy, and equanimity will guide my individual life, while our collective life will be based on sharing, pleasant language, constructive work, and equality.

Who Is William Arntz?

William Arntz began his professional sojourn as a research laser physicist. Two years was enough, and he left to explore the world. Along the way he became interested in the occult, eventually studying meditation with his first teacher, Rama—whose idea of a good time was to send his students into computer and entrepreneurial ventures. This culminated in Arntz writing a software product: AutoSys, which he sold to finance his retirement. With funds available he returned to an earlier passion, conceiving and creating the film *What the Bleep Do We Know!?* www.whatthebleep.com

BOOKS, MUSIC, AND MOVIES THAT HAVE INSPIRED WILL:

Shogun, James Clavell
All Carlos Castaneda's books
Handel's *Messiah*
Thunderheart
Ghost Busters

WILLIAM
ARNTZ

At some point in each of our lives we wake up to the fact that what we do has consequences. It seems in nature that the larger the organism, the longer it takes for that maturity to set in. So is it finally happening to the largest organism on Earth—Humanity? The fact that you read about Humanity as a (single) organism without missing a beat is telling: the notion of our connectedness has moved out of the realm of philosophy, into the realm of practical experience. Oh, it's happening. . . .

Who Is Angeles Arrien?

Angeles Arrien is the president of the Foundation for Cross-Cultural Education and Research. She lectures and conducts workshops worldwide, bridging cultural anthropology, psychology, and comparative religions. Ms. Arrien's work is currently used in medical, academic, and corporate environments. Her books, including *The Four-Fold Way*, *Signs of Life*, and *The Second Half of Life*, have been translated into nine languages, and she has received three honorary degrees in recognition of her work. www.angelesarrien.com

FIVE BOOKS THAT CONTINUE TO INSPIRE ANGELES'S LIFE:

Ethics for the New Millennium, H. H. the Dalai Lama
The Medici Effect, Frans Johansson
We Speak as One, edited by Arthur Zajonc
The Great Transformation, Karen Armstrong
Essential Spirituality, Roger Walsh

ANGELES
ARRIEN

Many perennial and indigenous wisdoms say that if we want to experience the "blessing way" in our family, in our work, and in our life, we must do three things every day:

• We must pray every day or set a sacred intention

• Give gratitude every day; this practice keeps the heart open

• Take a life-affirming action every day, through anonymous acts of kindness and generosity

If we want to have the experience of feeling connected to our own center, and to live the "blessing way," we have to do these things every day in order to walk the mystical path with practical feet.

Who Is Nic Askew?

Nic is many things. Filmmaker, storyteller, musician, composer. In his *Soul Biographies* short film series, he captures the experience of being human. And in doing so, offers viewers the opportunity to be moved to tears and laughter. And to move into a deeper experience of themselves. www.soulbiographies. com, www.nicaskew.com

BOOKS THAT HAVE INFLUENCED NIC GREATLY:

The Hobbit, J. R. R. Tolkien

The Alchemist, Paulo Coelho

Autobiography of a Yogi, Paramahansa Yogananda

NIC
ASKEW

A man had lived in his imagination. Ever since he was a boy.

For it was full of wonder and adventure when set against the outer world that housed his everyday life.

His imagination surrounded him in light. The outer world, in a darker shade. But as he waited for this outer world to catch the light, he realized that it might not.

And so he stepped out into the world, hand in hand with his imagination. Knowing that together they would bring light to the darkest of corners.

And he is you. And me.

And together, the imagination of our collective soul has already begun its inevitable work. As the light makes its way toward the experience of the world.

Who Is Mindy Audlin?

Mindy Audlin is an author, spiritual teacher, and founder of the "What If" Up! Club, helping expand mass consciousness through the applied power of imagination. She is the visionary behind Unity FM, a twenty-four-hour on-line spiritual broadcasting network, where she interviews world-renowned spiritual trailblazers as the host of her weekly talk show, *The Leading Edge*. www.whatifup.com, www.unity.fm

FIVE OF MINDY'S FAVORITE BOOKS:

The Prophet, Kahlil Gibran
The Alchemist, Paulo Coelho
Zero Limits, Joe Vitale
Discover the Power Within You, Eric Butterworth
The Path, Laurie Beth Jones

MINDY
AUDLIN

We are the chosen ones. We are blessed with the opportunity to midwife the birth of a new humanity. Together, we bring forth a world where the atrocities of war are footnotes in the history books of our children. Together, we engage in a technological revolution where compassion, appreciation, and interpersonal connections manifest in high speed and high definition! Together, we transcend the comfort of our feathered nests and take flight into a future of sustainability and abundance. The time is now. May all God's children, in glorious harmony, sing *together* the sacred anthem of *unity*.

Who Is Kenny Ausubel?

Kenny Ausubel is the founder and co-executive director of Bioneers, a non-profit educational organization that promotes practical environmental solutions and innovative social strategies for restoring the Earth and communities. He is an award-winning journalist, filmmaker, and social entrepreneur whose books include *The Bioneers: Declarations of Interdependence*, *When Healing Becomes a Crime: The Amazing Story of the Hoxsey Cancer Clinics and the Return of Alternative Therapies*. He cofounded Seeds of Change, a national biodiversity organic seed company, and founded Inner Tan Productions, a feature film development company. Kenny is also the executive producer and cowriter of the award-winning radio series: *Bioneers*. www.bioneers.org

FIVE BOOKS THAT HAVE SHAPED KENNY:

Biomimicry, Janine Benyus
Blessed Unrest, Paul Hawken
Utopian Legacies, John C. Mohawk
Wealth and Democracy, Kevin Phillips
A General Theory of Love, Thomas Lewis, Fari Amini, and Richard Lannon

KENNY
AUSUBEL

It's all alive—it's all connected—it's all intelligent—it's all relatives. The great work of this century is to apply these essential truths of the natural world as both practical and metaphoric guides for transforming human civilization to "create conditions conducive to life," in Janine Benyus's phrase. We didn't invent nature. Nature invented us. We would be wise to learn the ground rules and how to play by them. Scientists are affirming what the poets and mystics have known all along: We are all one. Beckoning us on is nothing less than the re-enchantment of the Earth.

Who Is Christina Baldwin?

Christina Baldwin is a writer, a global teacher, and a lifelong thought pioneer. At age thirty, she released her first book, *One to One*, which initiated the journal-writing movement. Her well-known classic, *Life's Companion,* defined journal writing as a spiritual practice. In the early 1990s, Baldwin and her partner, Ann Linnea, cocreated a group process that invokes the archetype of council expressed in modern terms. Her books *Calling the Circle, the First and Future Culture*; *The Seven Whispers: Spiritual Practice for Times Like These*; and *Storycatcher: Making Sense of Our Lives through the Power and Practice of Story* integrate her fascination with the role of story as a source of social activism. www.peerspirit.com, www.storycatcher.net

FIVE BOOKS THAT HAVE MOST INSPIRED CHRISTINA:

The Diary of a Young Girl, Anne Frank
Will and Spirit, Gerald G. May
The Walking People, Paula Underwood
New and Selected Poems, vols. 1 & 2,
    and everything else she's written, Mary Oliver
Deep Water Passage, Ann Linnea

CHRISTINA
BALDWIN

Stories build bridges: opinions build walls. When we know a person's story, we can find a way to see ourselves in one another. In a world where opinions rule, all sorts of false divisions are devised to separate us from our essential love of the other. But every person has the power to tell stories that expose our essential connection under all apparent differences. Generals and politicians plan the wars and divide the world, but *the people* have to live the consequences. Stories told in person, in writing, or on the Internet, leap over these walls and extend the possibility that we may find the heart of commonality. *What do you love most about the world?* Let's start there. Tell me that story.

Who Is Benjamin R. Barber?

Benjamin R. Barber is an internationally renowned political theorist and is currently a Distinguished Senior Fellow at Demos, where he is president of CivWorld, the international NGO that sponsors Interdependence Day and the Paradigm Project. Barber was the Walt Whitman Professor of Political Science at Rutgers University for thirty-two years, and then the Gershon and Carol Kekst Professor of Civil Society at the University of Maryland. A consultant with political and civic leaders in the United States and worldwide, Benjamin served as an informal consultant to President Bill Clinton. His seventeen books include the classic *Strong Democracy*, *Jihad vs. McWorld* and *Consumed: How Markets Corrupt Children, Infantilize Adults, Swallow Citizens Whole*, and *The Truth of Power: Intellectual Affairs in the Clinton White House*. Barber's honors are numerous and include a knighthood (Palmes Académiques/Chevalier) from the French government. Barber is a regular commentator for National Public Radio's *Marketplace*, and his blog can be found on The Huffington Post. He holds a certificate from the London School of Economics and Political Science and an MA and a Doctorate from Harvard University.

WORKS THAT HAVE HAD A MAJOR INFLUENCE ON BENJAMIN'S LIFE:
The Social Contract, Jean-Jacques Rousseau
Benito Cereno, Herman Melville
Democracy and Education, John Dewey
"Letter from Birmingham Jail," Martin Luther King, Jr.
In a Different Voice, Carol Gilligan

BENJAMIN R.
BARBER

The old aspiration? Independence. The new reality: interdependence. Every challenge we face today—from climate and crime, to technology and markets, to communications and public health—is global in character. Yet the institutions of democracy we rely on to address these challenges are still locked up inside sovereign states pursuing the old logic of independence. But in an interdependent world of diseases without borders, terrorists without borders, finance capital without borders, and war without borders, we also need citizens without borders—democracy without borders. Which means if we are to survive interdependence and flourish in liberty, we must either globalize democracy or democratize globalization.

Who Is Muhammad Abdul Bari?

Dr. Muhammad Abdul Bari is an educationalist with a PhD from King's College, London, and a management degree from the Open University. He has worked as an Air Force officer, a researcher in physics, a science teacher, and a SEN specialist in London. He is the former president of the Islamic Forum of Europe and is the chair of the East London Mosque Trust. He is a board member of the London Organising Committee of the Olympic Games Ltd and is a patron of the National Youth Agency and the Ramphal Centre for Commonwealth Policy Studies, London.

He has authored several books on parenting and on issues of youth and identity. These include: *Building Muslim Families*, *The Greatest Gift: A Guide to Parenting*, and *Race, Religion & Muslim Identity in Britain*. He was elected secretary general of the Muslim Council of Britain at its ninth annual General Meeting on June 4, 2006. Dr. Abdul Bari is married with four children.

FIVE WORKS THAT HAVE INSPIRED MUHAMMAD:
The Message of the Qur'an, Muhammad Asad
Inescapable Questions, Alija Izetbegovi
The Ornament of the World, María Rosa Menocal
Identity and Violence, Amartya Sen
The Muqaddimah, Ibn Khaldûn

MUHAMMAD **ABDUL** BARI

As a teacher, a parent, an author, a community worker, I keenly feel the need for an increased awareness of and understanding between our mosaic communities. In this restless age of natural and man-made calamities, wherein ever-increasing tensions, fears, and insecurities are seemingly paramount, we all strive toward solutions to give us hope and vision for life. We all seek to cultivate a society at ease with itself, free from fetters, to perform our duties on the basis of understanding and respect for human dignity. We all seek to develop our mental, emotional, physical, and spiritual strengths to better ourselves, our families, and our communities, and to add value to our society.

Who Is Glen Barry?

Dr. Glen Barry is a political ecologist, activist, and writer. He founded and runs the nonprofit Ecological Internet, which provides environmental portal services at www.ecoearth.info. There he writes the Internet's longest continuously running blog. www.climateark.org

BOOKS THAT HAVE IMPACTED GLEN'S LIFE:

War and Peace, Leo Tolstoy
Stranger in a Strange Land, Robert A. Heinlein
The Road, Cormac McCarthy
The Stand, Stephen King

GLEN
BARRY

Ecological crises are killing Earth, and good human futures require massive social and environmental change. Being will end if we do not strictly and lovingly protect and restore all rainforests, water, oceans, and atmosphere. Sustaining Gaia, the biosphere, ecosystems, biodiversity, and thus human habitat requires personal and societal sacrifice, including lower birthrates, less consumption, and an end to ancient forest logging and coal emissions. It is desired social change to avoid ecological collapse and social disintegration. Yet, should it be necessary, we must be prepared to fight an Earth revolution for global ecological sustainability.

Who Is Maggie Baxter?

Maggie is currently developing the first UK-wide Women's Fund; is producing an anti-trafficking film along with delivering gender training; and is undertaking other freelance work. In 2007 Maggie left her position as executive director of WOMANKIND Worldwide where she had worked since May 1999. Prior to this she was deputy chief executive and grants director at Comic Relief. She was seconded as acting chief executive to set up the Diana, Princess of Wales Memorial Fund. Maggie has also worked with the Baring Foundation, the Camden Council, and was the director of a settlement. She is a trustee of City Parochial Foundation, Trust for London, Hilden Charitable Fund, Women for Refugee Women, Dance United, and Green Belt Movement International.

FOUR BOOKS AND A SONG THAT HAVE INSPIRED MAGGIE:

Long Walk to Freedom, Nelson Mandela
Residence on Earth, Pablo Neruda
The Golden Notebook, Doris Lessing
The Prophet, Kahlil Gilbran
"We Shall Overcome," sung by Joan Baez

MAGGIE
BAXTER

Staggeringly extraordinary women! Those who against all odds challenge the status quo; those who do a hundred jobs a day and still have a smile on their faces; those who give their lives to supporting others, whether it be their sisters' children who have been orphaned by AIDS or as a result of civil war. Why do we still have to argue the case for women's opinions and experiences to be taken seriously? Women do their work as wives, mothers, grandmothers, carers, wood carriers, vegetable growers, street traders—they are not part of the statistics, they remain hidden—but they are the glue that holds our societies together. Invest in them, trust them, respect them.

Who Is Noah benShea?

Noah benShea is one of North America's most respected and beloved poet-philosophers. He is the international bestselling author of twenty-two books translated into eighteen languages, including the famed Jacob the Baker series embraced by millions around the world. In 2009 Noah was the subject of a National Public Television special and is the national laureate for the ALS Association. www.noahbenshea.com

A BOOK THAT HAS IMPACTED NOAH'S LIFE GREATLY:

One book more than any other has impacted his life and by which all other books pale: the Bible.

NOAH
BENSHEA

Imagine your life as a wagon filled with everything you represent, one where you need horses. Now imagine that your fears and your faith are those horses. Of course all of us have more fears than faith, so let us say we have eleven horses of fear and only one horse of faith. If we put any of the horses of fear at the head of the team, they will be hesitant to lead, unsure of their capacity, afraid they will not be able to do what is expected of them. But if you put the one single horse of faith as the lead, the horses of fear will follow. In fact, our fears, when led by our faith, will provide the strength to pull our wagon. The challenge for all of us is to put our faith and not our fears in charge.

Who Is Manju Bharat Ram?

Manju Bharat Ram is well-known for her involvement with education. She is the founder and chairperson of the innovative Shri Ram Schools in India, which were started in 1988 with the objective of developing each student's potential to the fullest. Her other responsibilities include being a founding member of Charity Aid Foundation, India (CAF), which was set up as part of the CAF International network; chairperson of Shriram Educare, a nonprofit consultancy working to transform school education; trustee and honorary general secretary of the Blind Relief Association; chairperson of SRF Vidyalaya, Chennai; and, being on the Board of Governors for Kendriya Vidyalaya Sangathan since 1998, an organization with over 800 schools. www.shriconnect.net

MANJU
BHARAT
RAM

Who better to invest in than children to lead us into a better future? Students of our school, which I founded, have heralded social awareness and change by being pro-active against environmental degradation and destruction, when explained to them the consequences.

Collecting money, they have helped in the rehabilitation and education of Mongiya tribal poachers, who were instrumental in the depletion of the tiger population; water conservation through rainwater harvesting, which has led to a rise in the water table; and emotional issues such as refraining from bursting firecrackers on Diwali festival.

Little, yet big steps … steps I rejoice being part of, for the future is theirs.

Who Is Michel Bitbol?

Michel Bitbol is a researcher in philosophy at the Centre de Recerche en Epistemologie Appliquée, Paris. He teaches epistemology at the University of Paris 1 Pantheon-Sorbonne. He was trained as a medical doctor, a physicist, and a philosopher. Michel first worked in biophysics and then turned to the philosophy of physics. He edited texts by Erwin Schrödinger and published *Schrödinger's Philosophy of Quantum Mechanics.* He also published books in French on quantum mechanics and on realism in science. Later, he focused on the philosophy of mind, working in close collaboration with Francisco Varela.

BOOKS THAT HAVE INSPIRED MICHEL:

Seraphita, Honoré de Balzac
An Interrupted Life, Etty Hillesum
The Fundamental Wisdom of the Middle Way, Nígírjuna
"Mind and Matter," Erwin Schrödinger
On Certainty, Ludwig Wittgenstein

MICHEL
BITBOL

One night, you trod a path edged with trees, wondering why that mischievous moon moved forward when you moved forward, and stopped when you stopped. This was childhood. Later on, you realized that the moon only *appears* to move, because it is far away and the trees are close to *you.* This was youth, and the excitement of objectivity: no wonder. But you have one more step to take. The step of disillusioned wonder, of full acceptance of the celestial show, with its laws and marvels, irrespective of the objective and the subjective. This would be adulthood.

Who Is Ryan Black?

Ryan Black founded Sambazon in 2000 after discovering the amazing açaí (ah-sigh-ee) fruit during a surfing trip to Brazil. Realizing that this fruit could become a powerful vehicle to spread a message of sustainable development, Ryan engineered a business model that would enrich the lives of thousands of local families, aid in the economic growth of the region, and protect the biodiversity of the Amazon rainforest through market-driven conservation. Prior to Sambazon, Ryan earned a finance degree at the University of Colorado, where he led the NCAA in tackles in 1996 as captain of the Buffaloe's nationally ranked football team. A social entrepreneur, Ryan is guided by the triple bottom line, which demonstrates that corporate success can be achieved on economic, social, and environmental levels. Most recently, Sambazon was named to the *Inc.* 500 and in 2006 won the prestigious Secretary of State Award for Corporate Excellence, presented by Condoleezza Rice. As chief executive of Sambazon, Ryan leads a new generation of social entrepreneurs who successfully use business to create positive economic change for the planet. www.sambazon.com

FOUR BOOKS AND A SONG THAT HAVE DEEPLY IMPACTED RYAN'S LIFE JOURNEY:

Let the Trumpet Sound, Stephen B. Oats

Bionomics, Michael L. Rothschild

Power vs. Force, David R. Hawkins

John Adams, David McCullough

RYAN
BLACK

Every day our purchases have a positive or negative effect on the lives of people globally. Market-based solutions, where people vote with their dollars, provide us as citizens the power to move mountains. We have the democratic system and intelligence to build a future based on positivity and prosperity. We have the power of innovation to leave negativity in the past and tackle society's biggest problems—poverty, conflict, and inequality. As citizens and brothers and sisters, we have a responsibility to participate in our democracy and create a future in which we want to live. Let's not let it be said that our generation refused to give up so little to gain so much.

Who Is Chrissie Blaze?

Chrissie Blaze is an international speaker, a regular media guest, astrologer, and teacher of metaphysics and the spiritual sciences. She is the author of many books, including *Power Prayer: A Program to Unlock Your Spiritual Strength; Workout for the Soul;* and *The Baby's Astrologer: Your Guide to Better Parenting Is in the Stars.* Blaze was a close student of the late Western Master of Yoga Dr. George King, who was president of the Aetherius Society. Chrissie is a priest and international synod member of the metaphysical organization King founded, and has been a senior healing instructor for over twenty years. Qualified as a lecturer at the University of London, she now lives in Los Angeles with her husband, author Gary Blaze. www.chrissieblaze.com

FIVE BOOKS THAT HAVE DEEPLY INSPIRED CHRISSIE:

The Nine Freedoms, Dr. George King

The Twelve Blessings, Dr. George King

Gods, Guides and Guardian Angels, Richard Lawrence

Autobiography of a Yogi, Paramahansa Yogananda

The Prophet, Kahlil Gibran

CHRISSIE
BLAZE

One of the most unifying visions we can have is the realization that we are all on planet Earth together. At the end of the day it is not our different belief systems that count, it is whether or not we will choose to destroy the beautiful Mother Earth that sustains us or heal our relationship to her. Let's raise our hands and hearts in prayer for the Earth and thank God for the priceless gift of continued experience she gives to us. Then let's work together as one human family in spiritual, charitable, and environmental ways to secure our future.

Who Is Karen Blincoe?

Karen Blincoe is a designer, educator, and environmentalist. She is the former director of the Schumacher College, Devon, a unique center for studies in sustainability issues based on Gandhian teaching and learning principles. Karen was educated in graphic design in the UK and established a graphic design consultancy in London. She became head of the Institute for Communication at the Danish Design College in 1992, and in 2001 she set up the International Centre for Creativity, Innovation, and Sustainability (ICIS) educational center in Denmark to teach and develop educational models for designers and architects in topics relating to sustainability, leadership, and business innovation. Karen has held many honorary positions, including chair of the Educational Council for the Arts, Design and Architecture in Copenhagen. Karen lectures on sustainability, design, and education around the world and also works with spiritual issues, personal development, leadership, and conflict solving. blincoe@iciscenter.org, www.iciscenter.org

FIVE WORKS THAT HAVE DEEPLY IMPACTED KAREN'S LIFE JOURNEY:

Initiation, Elisabeth Haich
The Externalisation of the Hierarchy, Alice Bailey (and all her other books)
The New Testament
The Tibetan Book of Living and Dying, Sogyal Rinpoche
The Prophet, Kahlil Gibran

KAREN
BLINCOE

The evolutionary process of humankind seems painfully slow, even though it is just a bleep, a fragment in Earth time.

I believe there are layers to human evolution. We are still at the outer layers, making mistakes, blundering along in our unconscious state. However, we occasionally catch a glimpse of what might be, what could be, and what we could become.

I want for us to move through to those inner layers where we live in oneness with ourselves, our communities, and our environment, so that the Earth doesn't need to shake us off too soon.

For this to happen we must have the courage and wisdom to deal with what's within.

Who Is William Bloom?

William Bloom, PhD, is one of the UK's best-known holistic educators and writers. He also dances, rides a motorbike, and lives with his family and many animals in Glastonbury. He is the founder of the Foundation for Holistic Spirituality; cofounder of the Alternatives Programme of St. James's Church, Piccadilly; and Fellow of the Findhorn Foundation. His many books include *The Endorphin Effect* and *Solution: The Holistic Manifesto.* www.williambloom.com

WORKS THAT HAVE CHANGED WILLIAM'S LIFE:

A Treatise on Cosmic Fire, Alice Bailey
The Immense Journey, Loren C. Eiseley
A Structural Theory of Imperialism, Johan Galtung
Seth Speaks, Jane Roberts
The Grapes of Wrath, John Steinbeck
The Yoga Sutras of Patañjali
The Gospels, New Testament

WILLIAM
BLOOM

I am touched and healed by the wonder of existence.

I do not understand its source, meaning, or intention—and am content with this unknowing.

My body and consciousness experience nature and the cosmos as benevolent, flowing, and emergent.

My primary, instinctual drive is to integrate this experience—benevolent, flowing, emergent—wholly into every aspect of myself.

My heart is joyful as I meet all those who share this instinct too.

I dedicate my life to supporting all beings, so that they may be free of suffering and liberated fully to enjoy their existence.

Who Is Alan Briskin?

Alan Briskin, PhD, is a consultant, speaker, and cofounder of the Collective Wisdom Initiative. His book *The Stirring of Soul in the Workplace* helped shape the spirit and work movement in the late 1990s. A leading voice in the organizational development field, he has aided businesses, health care, and nonprofit organizations to navigate change and renew organizational mission. His clients have included Kaiser Permanente, George Lucas Educational Foundation, and the Commonwealth Club of San Francisco. His coauthored book *Daily Miracles*, on the practice of nursing, was honored as Book of the Year by *The American Journal of Nursing* in 2008. www.alanbriskin.com

BOOKS THAT HAVE INSPIRED ALAN:
How to Change the World, David Bornstein
Nature and Other Writings (including the essay "The Over-Soul"),
    Ralph Waldo Emerson
Mountains Beyond Mountains, Tracy Kidder
The American Soul, Jacob Needleman
The Search for Common Ground, Howard Thurman

ALAN
BRISKIN

If I were to look at the future, I'd see the living envelope of life, our biosphere, becoming more fragile. As I scanned further, I would also note something else, an energy force surrounding the biosphere, crackling with a spiritual consciousness. In small groups and in millions of networks, actions that signified our collective potential would begin threading themselves across the planet. I would see a circle of humanity healing wounds and creating a future that honored the interconnectedness of life. These first millions would be heralds of a new consciousness. They would grasp the cocreative power of different groups with different interests acting together to solve problems collectively. Rather than seeing the group as a threat to individuality, they would form associations that respect human differences and individuals' talents. This would be collective wisdom.

Who Is Juanita Brown?

Juanita Brown, PhD, is the cofounder of the World Café, an innovative approach to large group dialogue now being used in corporate, community, government, health, education, NGO, and multi-stakeholder settings on six continents to engage conversations that matter across traditional boundaries. Juanita has served as a member of the MIT Dialogue Project, as a research affiliate with the Institute for the Future, and as a Fellow of the World Business Academy. Her award-winning book, *The World Café: Shaping Our Futures Through Conversations that Matter*, coauthored with David Isaacs and the World Café Community, illuminates key design principles for accessing mutual intelligence around complex issues. www.theworldcafe.com

FIVE BOOKS THAT HAVE INFLUENCED JUANITA'S LIFE AND WORK:

A Mantis Carol, Laurens Van der Post
Hope in the Dark, Rebecca Solnit
The Timeless Way of Building, Christopher Alexander
Complexity, M. Mitchell Waldrop
Shared Minds, Michael Schrage

JUANITA
BROWN

There is the possibility for a transformation of the nature of consciousness, both individually and collectively, and ... whether this can be solved depends on dialogue.
  —*David Bohm, physicist,* On Dialogue

We have the choice now to use our uniquely human gift for being in conversation together to foster authentic dialogue, access collective intelligence, and assure committed action around the questions that matter most—for our families, our organizations, our communities, and for future generations. This is the great opportunity of the twenty-first century if we are to survive and thrive together on this fragile and beautiful planet we call home. Yes, we can!

Who Is Lester Brown?

Lester R. Brown is an American environmentalist, founder of the Worldwatch Institute, and founder and president of the Earth Policy Institute, a nonprofit research organization based in Washington, D.C. Radio commentator Peter Day, of the BBC, said Lester is one of the great pioneer environmentalists. Brown is the author or coauthor of over fifty books on global environmental issues, and his works have been translated into more than forty languages. One of his most recent books is *Plan B 3.0: Mobilizing to Save Civilization*. Klaus Schwab of the World Economic Forum describes it as "a great book which should wake up humankind." www.earth-policy.org

BOOKS THAT HAVE IMPACTED ON LESTER'S LIFE:

Collapse, Jared Diamond
Silent Spring, Rachel Carson
The Man Who Planted Trees, Jean Giono
The Swiss Family Robinson, Johann David Wyss
The Collapse of Complex Societies, Joseph A. Tainter

LESTER R.
BROWN

The challenge today is to build a new economy and to do it at wartime speed before we miss so many of nature's deadlines that the economic system begins to unravel. The new economy will be powered by renewable energy, with a diverse transportation system employing light rail, buses, and bicycles, as well as cars, and have a stable population. The good news is that we already have the technologies to build it. We can move the world onto a path of sustained progress. The choice made by our generation will affect life on Earth for all generations to come.

Who Is Julia Butterfly Hill?

Julia Butterfly Hill is an American activist and environmentalist. Hill is best known for living in a 180-foot-tall, 600-year-old California redwood tree for 738 days between December 10, 1997, and December 18, 1999. Hill lived in the tree, affectionately known as Luna, to prevent loggers of the Pacific Lumber Company from cutting it down. She was presented the Courage of Conscience Award on October 31, 2002.

Hill is the author of the book *The Legacy of Luna: The Story of a Tree, a Woman, and the Struggle to Save the Redwoods* and coauthor of *One Makes the Difference: Inspiring Actions that Change Our World*. www.juliabutterflyhill.wordpress.com

BOOKS THAT INSPIRED JULIA'S LIFE:
Prison Writings: My Life Is My Sun Dance, Leonard Peltier
The Lorax, Dr. Seuss
Horton Hears a Who!, Dr. Seuss

JULIA
BUTTERFLY
HILL

"YOU BEING ME, BEING YOU"

You are a part of me, and I am a part of you.
When one reaches out to another, then one transforms to two.
But two is never separate from the one it was before.
If anything two is the possibility of one becoming more.
And if there were no counting, no numbers to create a wall,
when we looked in the face of one, we would see the face of all.
Can you imagine what our world would be like if we chose to see every
thought, word, and action through this lens—including the other-than-human
relatives that we share this Sacred Planet with?
The future is being created now.

Who Is Lucia Capacchione?

Lucia Capacchione is a registered art therapist, workshop leader, creativity coach, and bestselling author of thirteen books, including *Visioning: Ten Steps to Designing the Life of Your Dreams*, *Recovery of Your Inner Child,* and *The Creative Journal.* Her innovative methods spark and nurture creativity in all areas of life. She has been a consultant to Walt Disney Imagineering and is the director of Creative Journal Expressive Arts Training. www.luciac.com

LUCIA
CAPACCHIONE

Turning dreams into reality is child's play if you know the secret. And what's the secret? It's simple. Enter that childlike and naturally creative place in your heart and mind. The place where you daydream. The zone where you go when you are at your most creative. Find a quiet space and time for yourself and take some scissors, glue, paper, and old magazines to collage your heart's desire. Sounds like kindergarten stuff, doesn't it? But it truly begins there. Where we all began. As open, imaginative, and adventurous children wanting to explore all the possibilities life has to offer.

Who Is Tim Carpenter?

Tim Carpenter founded EngAGE, a nonprofit providing life-changing programs to thousands of low-income seniors, and the *Experience Talks* radio show. Prior to his entry into the senior services arena, Mr. Carpenter worked as a journalist and advertising copywriter and holds a Bachelor of Arts in journalism from San Francisco State University. He is a credentialed writing teacher who has been teaching creative writing for stage and screen to seniors for more than ten years. In 2008 Tim was elected an Ashoka Fellow for being one of the top social entrepreneurs in the world. www.engagedaging.org

FIVE BOOKS THAT HAVE INFLUENCED TIM GREATLY:

To Kill a Mockingbird, Harper Lee
The Catcher in the Rye, J. D. Salinger
Rabbit, Run, John Updike
Great Expectations, Charles Dickens
The Lay of the Land, Richard Ford

TIM
CARPENTER

There is a voice we should more often listen to—a voice we know in our hearts offers sage advice that can help us through dark times. It is the voice of experience. Luckily, we live in a time when people all over the world are recognizing more and more the value of our elders and the logic in a perspective from someone who has been around the block a few times. If ever there were a time to study history for the sole purpose of avoiding its repetition—here we are! So pull up a chair at the table, sit at the campfire, take a counter seat at the diner—and listen to those who know more than you. Experience talks. We just need to learn to listen.

Who Is Robin Casarjian?

Robin Casarjian is the founder and director of the Lionheart Foundation, sponsor of the National Emotional Literacy Projects for Prisoners and Youth-at-Risk. She is the author of *Houses of Healing: A Prisoner's Guide to Inner Power and Freedom.* Over sixty thousand copies have been donated to prisons throughout the United States, where it has changed the nature of programming in some of the country's most violent institutions. Robin is also a pioneer in the emerging area of forgiveness work and author of *Forgiveness: A Bold Choice for a Peaceful Heart.* www.lionheart.org

WORKS THAT HAVE INFLUENCED AND INSPIRED ROBIN:

"If You Only Knew" and "Forever in Love," Donna Marie Cary
A Course in Miracles, Foundation for Inner Peace
The works and writing of Carlos Castaneda
The books of Chögyam Trungpa Rinpoche

ROBIN
CASARJIAN

Vision ... a world where all people appreciate the value of taking time to go inward to be quiet and still each day—if only for a short time. Aligning with this stillness becomes as important to the human race as eating or sleeping. From this stillness and quiet, we come to know an inner peace and sense of safety that we recognize cannot be extinguished. From this, we access the compassion and boldness to extend love and forgiveness to all and take a stand for peace and justice in whatever small or large ways we are called to.

Who Is John Cavanagh?

John Cavanagh has been the director of the Institute for Policy Studies in Washington, D.C., since 1998 and is a founding fellow of the Transnational Institute (TNI) in Amsterdam.

Formerly an economist with the United Nations Conference on Trade and Development (UNCTAD) and the World Health Organization (WHO), he is the TNI Board of Trustees chair and sits on the executive committees of the U.S.-based Alliance for Responsible Trade and the Citizens' Trade Campaign. Cavanagh helped establish the International Forum on Globalization in 1995, and has been active in the anti-NAFTA networks. He works closely with the Progressive Caucus of the U.S. Congress and the international department of the U.S. trade union federation, the AFL-CIO, on corporate accountability and international labor rights. He is the coauthor of ten books and numerous articles on globalization. Cavanagh has a BA from Dartmouth College and an MA from Princeton. www.ips-dc.org

JOHN
CAVANAGH

The two greatest impediments to a more just and sustainable world are excess U.S. power and excess corporate power. Today, vibrant social movements, working together across borders, are providing both the vision and the specifics of alternatives to U.S.-dominated corporate globalization. These movements have helped elect governments that reject the corporate agenda in several Latin American nations, and this is a major step forward. The new great challenge to these movements and governments is speeding up the paradigm shift to healthier societies that drastically reduce greenhouse gas emissions in time to save the planet. There is still time.

Who Is Alli Chagi-Starr?

Alli Chagi-Starr is Green for All's senior community engagement strategist and was the event chair of the Dream Reborn Conference. She worked previously at Ella Baker Center, in Oakland, California, where she helped implement the Solutions Salon series and other large convenings, including the Social Equity track at the United Nations World Environment Day. Alli is also the cofounder of the eight-year-old Art in Action Youth Leadership Program, which offers uplifting programs for young urban artists. Her essays about innovative activism appear in *Democratizing the Global Economy, Global Uprising, Voices from the WTO, The Political Edge* and *How to Stop the Next War Now.* She facilitates seminars on developing creative tools for global/personal transformation and movement building. www.greenforall.org

WHAT MOST INSPIRES ALLI:

What's Going On?, Marvin Gaye
A People's History of the United States, Howard Zinn
Beloved, Toni Morrison
The Color Purple, Alice Walker
"Get Up, Stand Up," Bob Marley
Toni Cade Bambara's quote: "The role of the revolutionary artist
   is to make revolution irresistible."

ALLI
CHAGI-STARR

Creative expression ignites the highest manifestation of our humanity. Art reminds us of our purpose as a species: to cultivate compassion, beauty, and joy. The future is calling us to awaken our courage and our collective creativity. Through living lives of contribution, we can transform a way of being that is small and scared, and step into who we really are. Across the planet, we are weaving a rich tapestry of many visions for a just and sustainable world. We are the seed planters for the generations to come. May we shine a light bright enough to illuminate a world we will not see. And may the trees be strong and the fruit sweet for our children's children.

Who Are Grace and Alan Chatting?

Grace and Alan met in 1995 and married in 1999. They both work as therapists and life coaches. In 2001 they decided to manifest a center for personal development, a place where people can unwind, refocus, and formulate a progressive vision for their life. The Anam Cara Centre opened for business in 2005 in Spain. *Anam cara* is Gaelic for "soul friend." Alan and Grace divide their time between their work in Spain, Ireland, and the UK. www.plymouth-counselling.co.uk

ALAN AND GRACE'S FAVORITE BOOKS:

The Spectrum of Consciousness, Ken Wilber
Conscious Loving, Gay and Kathlyn Hendricks
Unstoppable, Adrian Gilpin
Homecoming, John Bradshaw

GRACE
AND **ALAN**
CHATTING

Grace: I believe we are all spiritual beings having a physical experience. My life purpose is to be a cocreator with God; to raise the consciousness of myself, my community, and therefore the world, by therapy, coaching, and writing. If we all become more conscious of what we do and why we do it, and seek to do it with all our heart, we are more likely to make healthy choices that are good for ourselves, our fellows, and the planet.

Alan: My mission is to be inspired, courageous, confident, healthy, and loving and to enjoy abundance and the desires of my heart. I help others to do the same, by counseling, coaching, teaching, and role modeling. I believe that if we all live the best life we can, we can add to the sum of human happiness and healthy progress.

Who Is Doc Childre?

Doc Childre is a leading, in-depth researcher of human consciousness, dedicated to bringing a wider understanding of the heart to the planet. He founded the Institute of HeartMath in 1991 to study stress and heart-brain interactions, architected the HeartMath system, and founded HeartMath LLC in 1998 to provide training programs and tools for empowering heart-based living to companies, hospitals, schools, health professionals, athletes, and individuals of all ages to improve performance, health, and well-being. In 2002 Doc founded Quantum Intech, Inc. to develop emotion-interactive technologies, including the award-winning Freeze-Framer® heart rhythm feedback system, the mobile emWave® Personal Stress Reliever, and intui-technologies® for decision making. Doc is the author of numerous books, including *The HeartMath Solution, From Chaos to Coherence,* and *Transforming Stress*. www.heartmath.org

DOC
CHILDRE

In the last few years, more people than ever, from different backgrounds and walks of life, are talking about the heart. Whether it's speak from the heart, listen to your heart, connect with the heart, or follow your heart, there is growing mention and energetic awareness of the importance of the heart in life's decisions. This desire for more heart is an escalating momentum, one that people are called to by the nudge of their own intuition and from an increased desire for the deeper connection and nurturing of spirit that comes from heart-based interaction.

For years, after charting the changing energies and dynamics on the planet, and the increasing stress levels, it's been part of my intentionality to facilitate the awakening of the heart's intelligence and, through scientific research, help bridge the intuitive connections between mind, heart, and spirit. The planetary shift is driven by the desire for individual and collective spirit integration. As planetary intelligence unfolds, more will realize that the heart is a natural portal for spirit integration, yet requires practice and a commitment to heart-based living. "Heart-based living" encompasses peoples' intentions and actions that express the qualities of the heart in daily life, resulting in a more compassionate and spirit-infused humanity.

Who Is Swati Chopra?

Swati Chopra is a writer based in New Delhi, India. She focuses on spirituality and religion in her work and is author of *Buddhism: On the Path to Nirvana*. For her book project on women and spirituality, she has received a fellowship from the Foundation for Universal Responsibility of H. H. the Dalai Lama. Swati's writing has appeared in journals in India and abroad, including *Resurgence* and *Tricycle: The Buddhist Review.* www.swatichopra.com

FIVE BOOKS THAT HAVE AFFECTED SWATI'S LIFE:

I Am That, Maurice Frydman
Siddhartha, Hermann Hesse
Freedom in Exile, H. H. the Dalai Lama
Bhagavad Gita
Old Path White Clouds, Thich Nhat Hanh

SWATI
CHOPRA

Of the many hopes that light up my heart when I think of our collective future, I choose one—an end to the suffering of duality, of otherness. Those who have glimpsed its true nature describe Reality as an uncompromising whole. An intermeshed network, a mass of interconnections. In our beings we carry the spark that links us with everything else. Looking at a world that fragments anew each day into boundaries between self and other, one hopes for a radical realization of connection, of shared humanity, of the oneness that embraces us all and is the ground upon which our common destiny unfolds.

Who Is Sonia Choquette?

Sonia Choquette, PhD, has been a world-renowned visionary and revolutionary psychic and teacher. She specializes in helping people see their soul's plan which leads to satisfying and successful lives. She is the author of ten bestselling books, including *The Psychic Pathway, Your Heart's Desire* and *Trust Your Vibes.* Educated at the University of Denver, and the Sorbonne, Paris, in addition to holding a doctorate in metaphysics, Sonia has been featured on ABC, NBC, and CNN as well as in *New Woman* magazine, *USA Today*, *The Chicago Tribune*, and *The London Times*. www.soniachoquette.com

BOOKS THAT HAVE DEEPLY INSPIRED SONIA'S LIFE:

The Nature of Personal Reality, Jane Roberts
The Artist's Way, Julia Cameron
Spiritual Dimensions of Psychology, Hazrat Inayat Khan
A Course in Miracles, The Foundation For Inner Peace

SONIA
CHOQUETTE

You are a Divine Immortal Being, a precious child of the universe.

You are spirit—fiery, heavenly Intelligence created by God, unlimited in nature. There is no 'spiritual' to become, as though there is something fundamentally flawed in you, which you must correct or overcome. You are only spirit to embrace, express, grow, love, and enjoy.

As a Divine child of the universe you are made only of love. Learn to love yourself as God does, fully, freely, and unconditionally. You are a Divine Creative Being, made of love, here on Earth to accept and master this truth.

Who Is Tarra Christoff?

Tarra Christoff, MA, is a coach, facilitator, and public speaker with a master's degree in soul-centered psychology. Tarra supports and inspires new paradigm leaders committed to catalyzing change in the world. Her approach integrates community building, the expressive arts, ritual, spirituality, and the power of imagination to heal the world. She has studied with Thich Nhat Hanh and emphasizes a spiritually engaged approach to social change. www.tarrachristoff.com

INSPIRATION FOR TARRA:

True Work, Justine Willis Toms and Michael Toms
For a Future to Be Possible, Thich Nhat Hanh
The Essential Rumi, translated by Coleman Barks
New Dimensions Media, newdimensionsmedia.org
Esalen Institute, www.esalen.org
Institute of Imaginal Studies, www.imaginal.edu

TARRA
CHRISTOFF

The soul of the world is calling for our leadership. Each of us has sacred gifts and medicine to offer our world. Each of us is a catalyst for social change. Together and individually, we are now being called to embrace a new paradigm for healing our global landscape and to create new models of leadership. To wholeheartedly embody these larger shifts that we wish to see in our world, we must marry our inner changes with outer changes. The veil of darkness asks our souls to go deep and experience the grief of the world so that we can engage our leadership from a place of depth and wisdom.

Now is also the time for creating and nourishing our communities. These vital supports will sustain us as we bring our gifts forward in a world that is hungry for them, but not always ready to receive them. We must be as shamans, walking between the old familiar structures and birthing the new ones. As we claim our leadership, our world asks us to remember indigenous wisdom and re-imagine the possibilities envisioned by great teachers such as Mahatma Gandhi and Martin Luther King. It is our individual and collective imagination that will carry us toward a future that beholds the birthing of a new paradigm.

Who Is Katy Clarke?

Katy Clarke is a published writer of poetry, nonfiction, fiction, and drama. She teaches creative writing and her specialist field is helping new writers toward publication. Katy has always had a passion for enabling writers to find their own personal writing voice and to gain confidence in newly learned writing skills. Recently, she held the post of chairperson at the internationally known Writers' Summer School in Swanwick, Derbyshire, UK. cathrine@cathrineclarke.orangehome.co.uk

FIVE BOOKS THAT HAVE INSPIRED KATY:

The Last Hours of Ancient Sunlight, Thomas Hartman
The Prophet, Kahlil Gibran
The Power of Now, Eckhart Tolle
The Bible

KATY
CLARKE

As a child on a seesaw, we learn about balance. We discover what sends us soaring too high, what brings us crashing to the ground.

Finding balance within ourselves is important.

For humanity to not only survive, but to thrive, finding balance is now more crucial than ever. For the well-being of our planet and for humanity.

For all time, we have known about consciousness and spirituality. But now, we are in extra time. The desire for change, for more weight in this direction, is at a new zenith. And love is the fulcrum, the absolute center point.

Who Is Andrew Cohen?

Andrew Cohen is an American spiritual teacher and philosopher widely recognized for his original contribution to the emerging field of evolutionary spirituality. Through his public talks, writings, and dialogues with leading thinkers, he has rapidly become a defining voice in a worldwide alliance of individuals committed to the transformation of consciousness and culture. Cohen founded the international organization EnlightenNext, as well as the award-winning magazine *What Is Enlightenment?* He is the author of *Living Enlightenment: A Call for Evolution Beyond Ego* and is currently working on a new release, *When God Falls from the Sky: A Spiritual Handbook for the 21st Century.* www.andrewcohen.org

FIVE BOOKS THAT INSPIRED ANDREW:

Integral Spirituality, Ken Wilber

Kundalini, Gopi Krishna

Autobiography of a Yogi, Paramahansa Yogananda

The Way of the White Clouds, Lama Anagarika Govinda

A Guide to Spiritual Life, Swami Brahmananda

ANDREW
COHEN

I am passionately committed to creating a revolution in consciousness and culture. It's urgent that we begin to define a new moral, philosophical, and spiritual context that will, in its depth and breadth of vision, be able to embrace the multidimensional nature of the human predicament in all its complexity at the beginning of the twenty-first century. Some bold pathfinders are already well along in that endeavor. But the most important part of this project, I feel, is actually being willing to transform ourselves, as individuals coming together for a higher purpose, so that more and more of us will be able to directly intuit the contours and parameters of this new context from the evolving edge of consciousness itself.

Who Is Edward Cornish?

Edward Cornish is the founder of the World Future Society and editor of its magazine *The Futurist*. Born in New York City in 1927, he trained as a reporter at the *Washington* (D.C.) *Evening Star* and later worked as a science writer for the National Geographic Society in Washington. Alarmed by the threat of thermo-nuclear war in the early 1960s, he became concerned and interested in finding better ways to anticipate future events—and perhaps find ways to prevent wars and build a better future for humanity.

In 1996 he published a newsletter about the future called *The Futurist* and distributed it free to other visionaries, including Buckminster Fuller. Cornish served as the World Future society's first president for thirty-eight years before retiring. He continues to work for the society as editor of *The Futurist*. Among his books are: *The Study of the Future: An Introduction to the Art and Science of Understanding and Shaping Tomorrow's World* and *Futuring: The Exploration of the Future*. He resides in Bethesda, Maryland. www.wfs.org

BOOKS THAT HAVE GIVEN GREAT INSPIRATION TO ED:

The Origin of Species, Charles Darwin

The Grapes of Wrath, John Steinbeck

Republic, Plato

The Razor's Edge, Somerset Maugham

The Idea of Progress, J. B. Bury

EDWARD
CORNISH

The future does not just happen to us. We ourselves create it by what we do and fail to do. We are, in fact, shapers of destiny—our own and the world's. Shaping destiny wisely requires foresight—the ability to forecast possible or probable future events so we can deal with them intelligently. The good news is that there now are scientific ways to anticipate many future events and prepare for them. In this way, we can build a better future for ourselves and generations to come.

Who Is Shirley Cramer?

Currently the chief executive officer of Dyslexia Action, the UK's leading provider of educational services and support for individuals with dyslexia and specific learning difficulties, Shirley has worked in leadership positions in the volunteer sector in both the United States and the United Kingdom and has lectured and published on the subject of public policy and special needs in both countries. She is the coeditor of *Learning Disabilities: Lifelong Issues.*

INFLUENTIAL BOOKS FOR SHIRLEY:

No Ordinary Time, Doris Kearns Goodwin
A Suitable Boy, Vikram Seth
The Power of Resilience, Robert Brooks, PhD, Sam Goldstein, PhD
The Wealth and Poverty of Nations, David S. Landes
Helping America's Families, Alfred J. Kahn

SHIRLEY **CRAMER**

We need to emphasize to children that everyone has talents and special skills that make each person unique. We have a tendency, in life and especially in our school systems, of focusing on children's difficulties and problems, rather than spending time finding their particular "islands of competence." Building on their strengths and talents, whether they are academic, practical, musical, or sports-related, enables individuals to cope better with their weaknesses. Nurturing children's skills and strengths will enable the development of confident, supportive adults.

Who Is Rod Crook?

Rod Crook, former head teacher, geologist, and foster caregiver, is very happily married with two children, one granddaughter, and an extended family of young people fostered over the past thirty-eight years. Now retired as head teacher of Cockwood Primary School in Devon, UK, which has long been recognized by Ofsted as outstanding, Rod still visits schools—teaching geology to primary-age children. He is also closely associated with the Wembworthy Residential Centre and leads children's environmental activities there.

SONGS THAT CHANGED ROD'S LIFE:
"Blowin' in the Wind," Bob Dylan
"We Shall Overcome," sung by Pete Seeger

BOOKS THAT CHANGED ROD'S LIFE:
The Origin of Species, Charles Darwin
1984, George Orwell
Che Guevara, Jon Lee Anderson

ROD
CROOK

Our children shape our future. The fetus that is not yet born cannot be blamed for what is happening to our world.

So we must ensure that all children receive a stimulating and challenging education that prepares them to shoulder responsibility for the stewardship of our fragile planet. Schools must become happy, secure places where the academic, practical, social, and emotional aspects of learning are given equal value; where new technologies enhance but do not replace teacher/child communication; where every child is treated as an individual and has the inalienable right to grow up in a world free from hunger and abuse.

Who Is David Crystal?

David Crystal has spent his life exploring language and languages. Brought up in Wales, he studied English language and literature at University College London, then went on to teach linguistics at Bangor and Reading universities. He is currently honorary professor of linguistics at Bangor. He published the first of his hundred or so books in 1964 and now works from his home in Holyhead, North Wales, as a writer, editor, lecturer, and broadcaster. Since leaving the full-time academic world in 1984, he has also worked in reference, as editor of the Cambridge and Penguin families of general encyclopedias, and is currently much involved in Internet analysis, developing sense-engine techniques for improving search-related activities. www.davidcrystal.com

LITERATURE THAT HAS INSPIRED DAVID'S LIFE:

The Use of English, Randolph Quirk

The Language Poets Use, Winifred Nowottny

Explorations in Shakespeare's Language, Hilda Hulme

The Art of Warfare in Biblical Lands, Yigael Yadin

Collected Poems, Dylan Thomas

DAVID
CRYSTAL

How do you explain a vision? Only through language—and languages. Each of the six thousand or so human languages provides a unique record of the community that uses it—and they are currently dying out at the rate of one every two weeks or so. This means that half the world's languages will have disappeared by the time this century is over. We urgently need to document disappearing languages, therefore—for once a language that has never been written down dies, it is as if it has never been. We also need to celebrate the languages that are secure, and help the communities that want their endangered languages to be revitalized. My hope is for a renewed awareness of the central importance of linguistic diversity in achieving peaceful coexistence, and I want to see language and languages placed center stage. A Nobel-like prize for language. Major artworks celebrating language. And a living museum of languages in every country. For a start.

Who Is John Dear?

John Dear is an internationally recognized voice for peace and nonviolence. A priest, pastor, peacemaker, and author, he served for years as the director of the Fellowship of Reconciliation, the largest interfaith peace organization in the United States. After September 11, 2001, he was a Red Cross coordinator of chaplains at the Family Assistance Center in New York and counseled thousands of relatives and rescue workers. John has traveled the war zones of the world, been arrested some seventy-five times for peace, and given thousands of lectures on peace. He writes a weekly column for The National Catholic Reporter at www.ncrcafe.org. His many books include: *Transfiguration, You Will Be My Witnesses, Living Peace, The Questions of Jesus, The God of Peace, Jesus the Rebel, Peace Behind Bars,* and *Disarming the Heart.* He lives in New Mexico. www.johndear.org

BOOKS THAT INFLUENCED JOHN'S LIFE:
The Life of Mahatma Gandhi, Louis Fischer
The Seven Storey Mountain, Thomas Merton
The Long Loneliness, Dorothy Day
To Dwell in Peace, Daniel Berrigan
Strength to Love, Martin Luther King, Jr.

JOHN
DEAR

The future of humanity is a future of peace. That is our hope. War is not inevitable; nuclear destruction need not be our destiny; poverty and global warming can be stopped. We have to envision a new world without war, poverty, or nuclear weapons, and work for its coming. That means, we need to become people of active nonviolence, and move our culture from blindness to vision, violence to nonviolence, injustice to justice, war to peace. We can do it, but every one of us needs to work for disarmament and justice, and become a visionary of peace, a real peacemaker.

Who Is Bas de Leeuw?

Bas de Leeuw is head of Integrated Resource Management for the United Nations Environment Programme (UNEP), based in Paris. He has initiated a worldwide movement based on exploring and achieving sustainable consumption and production patterns. He has worked for the Organization for Economic Co-operation and Development (OECD) and for the Dutch government in the fields of macroeconomic, energy, and environmental policy planning. He has also been a journalist and a writer. Bas has a master's degree in macroeconomic policy from the Erasmus University, Rotterdam. www.unep.fr/sustain

BOOKS AND SONGS THAT HAVE MOST INSPIRED BAS'S LIFE:

What the Buddha Taught, Walpola Rahula
The Fountainhead, Ayn Rand
Demian, Herman Hesse
"Run, Baby, Run," Sheryl Crow
"There Ain't No Cure for Love," Leonard Cohen
"Beautiful People," Mathilde Santing
"Unchained Melody," Righteous Brothers
"Imagine," John Lennon

BAS DE
LEEUW

Sustainability is not about fighting against the waves of technology, industry, and economics. It is about riding them and determining ourselves where we land. The creativity, the knowledge, and the resources are at hand. It is time to answer. Do consumers have to go on blindly satisfying their desires, while looking away from the poor and helpless who sink deeper and deeper? We have the choice between consuming and caring. That vision gives power. It will bring about a new world. We will be reconnected with nature, with other people, and with ourselves. Now let us dare to move.

Who Is Christian de Quincey?

Christian de Quincey, PhD, is a professor of philosophy and consciousness studies at John F. Kennedy University, faculty member at the Graduate Institute, director of the Center for Interspecies Research, faculty member at the University of Philosophical Research and the Holmes Institute, and visiting faculty at Schumacher College, UK. He is also the cofounder of the Visionary Edge, committed to transforming global consciousness by transforming mass media. Dr. de Quincey is the author of the award-winning books *Radical Nature* and *Radical Knowing,* as well as the visionary novel *Deep Spirit.* www.deepspirit.com

FIVE BOOKS THAT HAVE HELPED TO SHAPE CHRISTIAN'S LIFE:

The Ghost in the Machine, Arthur Koestler
The I Ching or Book of Changes, translated by
    Richard Wilhelm & Cary F. Baynes
Science and Civilisation in China, vol. 2, Joseph Needham
The Tao of Physics, Fritjof Capra
The Reenchantment of Science, edited by David Ray Griffin

CHRISTIAN DE
QUINCEY

Fourteen billion years ago, it all started with a Big Bang. Today, all we hear is a faint echo. For centuries, scientists have been listening to the skies and have heard nothing but the constant rhythms of the stars spinning through space. The distant galaxies talk to us, but to the ears of science they speak only of chaotic fires, explosive hells of dead matter. Random noise, meaningless cosmic chatter. Yes, we live in an unimaginably vast universe, with countless billions of galaxies, stars, and planets. There must be—there is—intelligent life out there. We are not alone.

Who Is Louise DeSalvo?

Louise DeSalvo is the Jenny Hunter Professor of Creative Writing at Hunter College, New York. She has earned the Douglas Society Medal and the Gay Talese Award. DeSalvo has published sixteen books, among them, *The Letters of Vita Sackville-West and Virginia Woolf* and *The Milk of Almonds.* Her book *Virginia Woolf* was named an important book of the twentieth century by *Women's Review of Books.* She has also published the memoirs *Vertigo, Breathless, Adultery,* and *Crazy in the Kitchen,* named a Booksense Book of the Year for 2004. *Writing as a Way of Healing* is widely used by writers recovering from trauma and illness.

FIVE FAVORITE BOOKS THAT INSPIRED LOUISE:
Trauma and Recovery, Judith Herman
The Wounded Storyteller, Arthur W. Frank
The Artist's Way, Julia Cameron
The Courage to Write, Ralph Keyes
Fearless Creating, Eric Maisel

LOUISE
DESALVO

I would like to see a time when ordinary people, not just writers, use writing to reflect upon their lives—obstacles they've overcome, choices they've made, decisions they perhaps regret, joys they've had, pain they've experienced. This writing might begin in private in a journal; but, in time, the writer might choose to share the work with others, through "writing circles" that would function like book groups do. The writer might choose, too, to leave the work to the next generation, so each family could have a record of its origins and could garner wisdom from its elders.

Who Is Stephen Dinan?

Stephen Dinan is the director of membership and marketing at the Institute of Noetic Sciences and the creator of its Shift in Action membership program. He is also the editor of *Radical Spirit: Spiritual Writings from the Voices of Tomorrow*. Stephen directed and helped to create the Esalen Institute's Center for Theory & Research, a think tank for leading scholars, researchers, and teachers to explore human potential frontiers. Stephen is the author of more than one hundred articles and several books in self-development, including "Sacred America," *In Kali's Garden*, and *Angelfire*. www.stephendinan.com, www.shiftinaction.com

FIVE BOOKS THAT HAVE SHAPED STEPHEN'S LIFE:

Grace and Grit, Ken Wilber

The Adventure of Self-Discovery, Stanislav Grof

Initiation, Elizabeth Haich

Diet for a New America, John Robbins

Zen and the Art of Motorcycle Maintenance, Robert Pirsig

STEPHEN
DINAN

We are between eras, leaving a time in which the mind triumphed over nature, spinning a web of separation that led to nations, religions, and races each vying for supremacy, moving to a time in which our interconnection with each other becomes so real that we can no longer exclude anyone from our family. The clash of nations will give way to one planetary civilization. Schisms between religions will dissolve in one spirit. Our addiction to war will be eased by spreading peace. This emerging world will be built on a new understanding of what is sacred: our families, our flesh, our pain, our dreams, and our fears. All will shimmer with divine grace.

Who Is Janaia Donaldson?

Janaia Donaldson is the host of the *Conversations* series on Peak Moment TV, showcasing first-person stories and perspectives for locally reliant living in response to energy, climate, and economic challenges. With her partner, Robin, she lives in the Sierra Nevada foothills of California on 160 acres of forestland protected from development by conservation easements. She is a "layerist" artist whose paintings blend imagery of the microcosm, macrocosm, nature, Earth, and spirit. www.peakmoment.tv, www.janaia.com

FOUR BOOKS AND A MOVIE THAT HAVE INSPIRED JANAIA:

Small Is Beautiful, E. F. Schumacher

A Door into Ocean, Joan Slonczewski

The Spell of the Sensuous, David Abram

Your Money or Your Life, Joseph Dominguez and Vicki Robin

Harold and Maude

JANAIA
DONALDSON

A VIEW FROM THE FUTURE:

Our ancestors plunged into the twenty-first century on the surging wave of infinite material growth. They were experts at Big: population, production, consumption, waste, pollution.

They collided with our finite planet's limits to growth. Rapidly declining resources and ecosystems cascaded planetwide, resoundingly punctuated by the effects of climate chaos.

There are fewer of us now. We live small and local. Precious global links maintain our human communications. We are living into the restorative story, reweaving the myriad connections to the one we rely upon—Earth and her life-web. While we live within physical limits, we explore the infinite possibilities in being, beauty, art, music, spirit, play, wisdom, and reveling in nature's wondrous web.

Who Is Barbara Dossey?

Barbara Dossey, PhD, RN, AHN-BC, FAAN, internationally recognized as a pioneer in the holistic nursing movement, is the director of Holistic Nursing Consultants in Santa Fe, NM, and international codirector of the Nightingale Initiative for Global Health (NIGH), in Ottawa, Canada, and Washington, D.C. She is the author or coauthor of twenty-three books. Today her focus is holistic/integral nursing, compassionate care of the dying, and the Nightingale Declaration Campaign (NDC), an initiative to declare 2010: International Year of the Nurse and 2011–2020: UN Decade for a Healthy World. www.nightingaledeclaration.net

FIVE BOOKS THAT HAVE HELPED TO SHAPE BARBARA'S LIFE:
Cloud-Hidden Whereabouts Unknown, Alan Watts
C. G. Jung and Hermann Hesse, Miguel Serrano
Zen Mind, Beginner's Mind, Shunryu Suzuki
The Life of Florence Nightingale, Sir Edward Cook
Integral Psychology, Ken Wilber

BARBARA
DOSSEY

Our combined capacities in collaborative endeavours can heal the Earth and its people. With NIGH, I unite with nurses and concerned citizens of the global community to declare our willingness to unite in a program of action, to share information and solutions, and to improve health conditions for all humanity—locally, nationally, and globally. We can resolve to adopt personal practices and to implement public policies in our communities and nations—making this goal achievable and inevitable by the year 2020, beginning today in our own lives, in the life of our nations, and in the world at large.

Who Is Larry Dossey?

Dr. Larry Dossey is a physician of internal medicine, formerly with the Dallas Diagnostic Association. He is the former chief of staff of Medical City Dallas Hospital. He received his MD degree from Southwestern Medical School in Dallas, Texas, and trained in internal medicine at Parkland and the VA hospitals in Dallas. Dossey has lectured at medical schools and hospitals throughout the United States and abroad. In 1988 he delivered the annual Mahatma Gandhi Memorial lecture in New Delhi, India, the only physician ever invited to do so. He is the author of ten books, including the *New York Times* bestseller *Healing Words: The Power of Prayer and the Practice of Medicine* and most recently *The Extraordinary Healing Power of Ordinary Things*. Dr. Dossey is the former cochairman of the Panel on Mind/Body Interventions at the National Center for Complementary and Alternative Medicine, National Institutes of Health. He is the executive editor of the peer-reviewed journal *Explore: The Journal of Science and Healing.* Dr. Dossey lectures around the world. He lives in Santa Fe with his wife, Barbara, who is a nurse-consultant and the author of several award-winning books. www.dosseydossey.com

FIVE BOOKS THAT HAVE HELPED SHAPE LARRY'S LIFE:

The Medium, the Mystic, and the Physicist, Lawrence LeShan
The Spectrum of Consciousness, Ken Wilber
Quantum Questions, Ken Wilber
The Perennial Philosophy, Aldous Huxley
The Way of Zen, Alan Watts

LARRY
DOSSEY

A new vision of consciousness is arising within science that is radically different from the brain-based version that has dominated for centuries. Evidence from healing research compellingly suggests that consciousness is *nonlocal*—that is, it is *infinite* in space and time, therefore immortal and eternal. Although consciousness can work through the brain, it is not identical to it. Our thoughts and intentions can effect changes at a distance and unite seamlessly with other minds. The implications of this new vision are as majestic as the old view is dismal. It now appears that the universe is alive and filled with consciousness, and that we truly, genuinely *belong*.

Who Is Bill Drayton?

Bill Drayton is a social entrepreneur and founder/chairman and CEO of Ashoka. He is also chair of Youth Venture, Community Greens, and Get America Working! As a student, he was active in civil rights and founded a number of organizations ranging from Yale Legislative Services to Harvard's Ashoka Table. In 1970 he graduated from Yale Law School and began his career at McKinsey and Company in New York. From 1977 to 1981, Mr. Drayton served as assistant administrator at the U.S. Environmental Protection Agency (EPA), where he launched emissions trading (the basis of Kyoto) among other reforms. After the EPA, he returned to McKinsey part-time and launched Ashoka, Save EPA, and its successor, Environmental Safety. When he was elected a MacArthur Fellow in 1984, he devoted himself fully to Ashoka.

Drayton has won numerous awards and honors, including being selected in 2005 as one of America's Best Leaders by *U.S. News & World Report* and Harvard's Center for Public Leadership. In 2006 he was recognized as one of Harvard University's 100 Most Influential Alumni. www.ashoka.org

BOOKS THAT BILL HAS FOUND POWERFUL:
The Achieving Society, David C. McClelland
A Short History of Ethics, Alasdair MacIntyre
Genghis Khan and the Making of the Modern World, Jack Weatherford
Gandhi, Susanne Hoeber Rudolph and Lloyd I. Rudolph
Fist Stick Knife Gun, Geoffrey Canada

BILL
DRAYTON

The world has embarked on its biggest architectural change since the agricultural revolution's tiny surplus freed only a small elite.

Today we must break out to an "everyone a change-maker" world. As the number of institutions and how fast they need to change multiplies, this is the only way (1) solutions can outrun the problems and (2) people can be full citizens. Everyone needs to push. All young people must grasp empathy/teamwork/leadership—by practicing and practicing and therefore knowing they are change-makers before the age of twenty-one. The entrepreneurs then launch the new waves, and are both role models for and mass recruiters of the thousands of local change-makers they need to succeed.

Who Are Yvonne and Rich Dutra-St. John?

Motivated by memories of their own teen experiences and fueled by a desire to work for positive change, Yvonne and Rich Dutra-St. John created the award-winning Challenge Day program in 1987. Through their years of professional experience with teens and families, Rich and Yvonne recognized that oppression, bullying, and violence are actually symptoms of greater social problems: separation, isolation, and loneliness. Rich and Yvonne designed the Challenge Day program to build connection and forgiveness between youth, and to inspire teens to become positive forces of change in their schools and communities. Today, Challenge Day has touched the lives of hundreds of thousands of youth across North America and around the world. Rich and Yvonne have received numerous awards for their transformational work. In 2005 they were honored as Champions of Forgiveness by the Worldwide Forgiveness Alliance. Their work with Challenge Day has been featured in the Emmy Award—winning documentary *Teen Files: Surviving High School*, on *The Oprah Winfrey Show*, and in the Canadian documentary *The Bully Solution.* www.challengeday.org

FIVE BOOKS AND SONGS THAT HAVE INSPIRED YVONNE AND RICH:

Way of the Peaceful Warrior, Dan Millman
Man's Search for Meaning, Viktor E. Frankl
How to Talk so Kids Will listen & Listen so Kids Will Talk,
    Adele Faber and Elaine Mazlish
"Love, Serve, and Remember," John Astin
"Where Is the Love," Black Eyed Peas

YVONNE **AND** RICH **DUTRA-ST. JOHN**

Borrowing the words of Mahatma Gandhi, we believe we must be the change we wish to see in the world. By demonstrating that love, acceptance, and compassion are possible for all people, we envision a world where every child—including the child inside each one of our hearts—feels safe, loved, and celebrated. Imagine a world where each parent would ask him- or herself, "Will what I'm about to say or do leave my kids feeling safe, loved, and celebrated?" Or before making any decision, every politician, government official, and person in power on this planet would ask him- or herself, "Will the choice I'm about to make leave the people of this world feeling safe, loved, and celebrated?" That would be peace on Earth!

Who Is Riane Eisler?

Raine Eisler is best known for her international bestseller *The Chalice and the Blade* and her award-winning *Tomorrow's Children*, *Sacred Pleasure*, and *The Power of Partnership*. Her latest book, *The Real Wealth of Nations: Creating a Caring Economics,* was hailed by Archbishop Desmond Tutu as "a template for the better world we have been so urgently seeking" and by Jane Goodall as "a call to action." Dr. Eisler is president of the Center for Partnership Studies, has taught at the University of California, and has expanded the vision of international human rights organizations to include the rights of women and children. She keynotes conferences worldwide and is a consultant to businesses and government agencies on applications of the partnership model introduced in her work. www.partnershipway.org, www.rianeeisler.com

FOUR BOOKS THAT INSPIRED RIANE TO SEARCH MORE DEEPLY:
Living My Life, Emma Goldman
The Age of Voltaire, Ariel and Will Durant
Sexual Politics, Kate Millett
Darwin's Lost Theory, David Loye

RIANE
EISLER

When my first grandchild was born, I became even more passionate about cultural transformation. Children have an enormous capacity for love, creativity, and joy. But for them to realize these potentials, we must build cultures where mutual respect and caring, rather than top-down rankings of domination, are supported in all relations—from intimate to international. We must pay special attention to the primary human relations: the relations between the female and male halves of humanity and between parents and children—where people first learn respect for human rights or where they no longer accept human rights violations as "just the way things are." Then we will have solid foundations for a more just, caring, and sustainable future.

Who Is Duane Elgin?

Duane Elgin, MBA, MA, is an internationally recognized speaker and author. His books include: *Promise Ahead*, *Voluntary Simplicity*, and *Awakening Earth*. He has worked as a senior staff member on the Presidential Commission on the American Future and as a senior social scientist with the think tank SRI International, where he coauthored numerous studies of the future. One such book was coauthored with Joseph Campbell. In 2006 Duane received the international Goi Peace Award in recognition of his contribution to a global "vision, consciousness, and lifestyle" that fosters a "more sustainable and spiritual culture." www.awakeningearth.org

FIVE BOOKS THAT HAVE INFLUENCED DUANE GREATLY:

Cosmic Consciousness, Richard Bucke
The Spirit of Zen, Alan Watts
The Buddhist Teaching of Totality, Garma Chang
The Power of Myth, Joseph Campbell with Bill Moyers
Mysticism, Evelyn Underhill

DUANE
ELGIN

Where are we? We live within a living universe that arises, moment by moment, as a unified whole. The entire universe is being regenerated completely in a continuous flow. We are inseparable from this flow. *Who are we?* We are beings of both biological and cosmic dimension. When we come to our center, we experience ourselves as flow-through beings who are continually emerging from the living universe. *Where are we going?* We are on a grand journey of awakening to our invisible aliveness. The universe is a learning system, and we are students of eternity. Let's get on with the adventure!

Who Is John Elkington?

Cofounder of SustainAbility in 1987, John Elkington is a world authority on corporate responsibility and sustainable development. In 2004 *BusinessWeek* described him as "a dean of the corporate responsibility movement for three decades." SustainAbility is based in London, Zurich, and Washington, D.C. John has authored or coauthored seventeen books, including 1988's million-selling *The Green Consumer Guide* and *Cannibals with Forks: The Triple Bottom Line of 21st Century Business*. His latest book, coauthored with Pamela Hartigan of the Schwab Foundation, is *The Power of Unreasonable People*. www.sustainability.com, www.johnelkington.com

BOOKS AND WORKS THAT HAVE GIVEN JOHN HOPE:

Silent Spring and *The Sea Around Us,* Rachel Carson
Dune, Frank Herbert
The entire output of James (Jim) Lovelock, including *Gaia*
Our Common Future, The World Commission on Environment
    and Development (Brundtland Commission)
The Green Consumer Guide, John Elkington and Julia Hailes

JOHN
ELKINGTON

Visions have illumined my life in many ways. Teachers, songs, poems, books, films, paintings, sculptures, the occasional life-shaping dream, and, yes, hallucinatory drugs in the 1960s. But the most profound evolved in conversation. Indeed, one of the unending joys of the environmental and sustainability movements is how many truly inspirational people there are in the conversation. Some years ago, in Sydney, I was asked during a plenary debate what SustainAbility's most powerful strategic tool was. Without hesitation, I replied, "our sofa." These days, we have several, but it's more true than ever. The most enduring visions are coevolved and shared.

Who Is Michele Elliott?

Michele Elliott is a teacher and psychologist and the author of twenty-five books translated into sixteen languages. She is the founder of the award-winning children's charity Kidscape, which was the first charity in the UK to deal with the prevention of sexual abuse and bullying. She has chaired World Health and Home Office Working Groups, is a Winston Churchill Fellow and was awarded an OBE that she insists is for the entire Kidscape staff, which works so hard to keep children safe. She has been married for over forty years to a teacher and is the mother of two sons. www.kidscape.org.uk

FIVE BOOKS THAT HAVE UPLIFTED MICHELE:

To Kill a Mockingbird, Harper Lee
It's Not About the Bike, Lance Armstrong
Ten Fun Things to Do Before You Die, Karol Jackowski
A Midwife's Tale, Laurel Thatcher Ulrich
The Adventures of Huckleberry Finn, Mark Twain

MICHELE
ELLIOTT

Working in a small children's charity, the problems and difficulties often seem overwhelming. You cannot save all the children, and discouragement sets in when the cases seem endless—it is like bailing out the ocean with a bucket. But I have learned to keep bailing into a pool behind me, which is getting bigger every day. One more child saved, and another and another. . . .

When any problem seems insurmountable, start bailing one bucket at a time, turn away from the ocean and look at the pool. One more problem gone and another and another. . . .

Who Is Edzard Ernst?

Professor Ernst qualified as a physician in Germany, where he also completed his MD and PhD theses. He was a professor in Physical Medicine and Rehabilitation (PMR) at Hanover Medical School in Germany and head of the PMR Department at the University of Vienna. In 1993 he came to the University of Exeter as the first chair in Complementary Medicine. He is the founder/editor-in-chief of two medical journals: *FACT (*Focus on Alternative and Complementary Therapies) and Perfusion. Ernst's work has earned him twelve scientific prizes/awards and two visiting professorships. He served on the Medicines Commission of the British Medicines and Healthcare Products Regulatory Agency, and on the Scientific Committee on Herbal Medicinal Products of the Irish Medicines Board. In 1999 he took British nationality. To date he has published over thirty-nine books and more than one thousand peer-reviewed papers and delivered over five hundred international lectures. www.pms.ac.uk/compmed

EDZARD
ERNST

In my field, complementary/alternative medicine, the visionary bench is overcrowded and the scientists' corner feels deserted. Personally I prefer the company of scientists. Scientists are no prophets. Instead of speculating about the future, they prefer to labor toward improving it. If we want to render tomorrow's health care better than today's, we need more people in complementary/alternative medicine who are capable of rational thinking and fewer who indulge in utopian pipe dreams, more who establish an evidence base and fewer who insist on double standards. Perhaps that already is a vision.

Who Is Esateys?

Esateys is a nationally Board Certified nurse practitioner. She is a pioneer, international lecturer, and spiritual teacher in the fields of energy medicine and awakening human consciousness. After her near-death experience in 1981, her inner knowing awakened. This heightened consciousness allowed her to see Life as the illusionary Game that it truly is. She has supported people in identifying and dissolving the blocks that lead to disease, illness, pain, and suffering.

Esateys is a cohost of the weekly Internet radio show *Relationships and Beyond*. She is the author of *Help! I'm Trapped in a Body! The Power of the Total Body Matrix*^{sm} and *Jumping Off the Chessboard, Waking Up from the Game Called Life* (working title) and has produced many CDs featuring her message and teachings. www.esateys.com

FIVE BOOKS THAT HAVE TOUCHED ESATEYS'S SOUL:
The Way of Mastery, Shanti Christo Foundation
The Power of Now, Eckhart Tolle
The Bhagavad Gita for Daily Living, vols. 1, 2, 3, Eknath Easwaran
A Course in Miracles, Foundation for Inner Peace
Busting Loose, Robert Scheinfeld

ESATEYS

Life is a game. It's all an illusion. Our quest is to make known the unknown and live Life fully awake and aware. The world is based on the polarity of Love versus Fear. Love is all there is. Fear is what keeps "The Game" alive and active. The magical key to freedom is to welcome the fear and all resistance that comes your way. When there is no resistance, polarity and fear cease. Freedom follows. When we are truly present in each moment and accept "what is" (without resistance) we change our world.

Who Is Martha Farnsworth Riche?

The honorable Martha Farnsworth Riche, PhD, was director of the U.S. Census Bureau between 1994 and 1998, maintaining the line of directors of the world's oldest continuous census which began in 1790 with Thomas Jefferson. A Fellow at the Center for the Study of Society and Economy at Cornell University, Dr. Riche consults, writes, and lectures on demographic changes and their effects on policies, programs, and products. She is also a Fellow of the American Statistical Association and a trustee of Redefining Progress, an organization dedicated to finding commonsense solutions to issues of sustainability. www.farnsworthriche.com, www.rprogress.org

FIVE BOOKS THAT HAVE TRANSFORMED AND EXPANDED MARTHA'S WORLDVIEW:

Eccentric Spaces, Robert Harbison
A la Recherche du Temps Perdu, Marcel Proust
The Feminine Mystique, Betty Friedan
The Second Sex, Simone de Beauvoir
The Structures of Everyday Life, Fernand Braudel

MARTHA
FARNSWORTH
RICHE

Three normally hostile peoples briefly created a vibrant civilization in twelfth-century Sicily. The Norman architecture, Saracen arches, and Byzantine mosaics of Palermo's Cappella Palatina are its visual legacy. In the twentieth century, empirical research validated this "business case" for diversity: diverse work groups that can communicate and handle conflict productively produce superior solutions. This is the challenge of the twenty-first century. As the world's population stabilizes at a billion or more people than at present, economic (and thus political) power becomes more widely distributed, and countries become increasingly interdependent. How well we work with "others" will determine the world's future.

Who Is Edie Farwell?

Edie is the program director of the Donella Meadows Leadership Fellows Program at the Sustainability Institute. She has an MA in cultural and social anthropology from the California Institute of Integral Studies and a BA in anthropology and environmental studies from Dartmouth College. She was the director of the Association for Progressive Communications and co-led the APC multicultural team at the 1992 United Nations Earth Summit in Brazil; led the communications installation at the 1993 UN World Conference on Human Rights in Austria; and managed a global team of forty women to provide Internet installation, training on strategic use, and information dissemination at the 1995 UN World Conference on Women, China. She lives with her family at the eco-village Cobb Hill Co-housing in Vermont. www.sustainer.org

BOOKS AND POEMS THAT HAVE INSPIRED EDIE:
City of Joy, Dominique Lapierre
Midnight's Children, Salman Rushdie
The Last Report on the Miracles at Little No Horse, Louise Erdrich
The Animal Family, Randall Jarrell
Things Fall Apart, Chinua Achebe
"The Guest House," Rumi
"Wild Geese," Mary Oliver

EDIE
FARWELL

My vision is that each individual has the ability to discover their innate talents and passions, and to contribute these gifts in service of global sustainability. I dream of a respectful, healthy interaction between the Earth and its inhabitants, where most all people, in my country and in most all other countries, are doing all we can to conduct ourselves and our lifestyles to be life-sustaining. As we deplete our Earth's resources of clean air, pure water, robust forests, and social capital, and as global warming gains momentum, it will take everything we have and most everybody's contributions to reverse these trends and secure a substantial shift to global sustainability. Together we can do it.

Who Is Miriam Feist?

Miriam Feist, born Zaremba, is the cofounder of both 54Success, an international company for transformation and lean management, and the Mind & Business Institute, which offers effective Buddhist methods for entrepreneurs and managers.

She worked for a German publishing house in the fields of integral leadership and future business ethics as well as serving as the director in Germany of the World Future Council.

Being a Buddhist practitioner since 1996, she engages herself in the international nonprofit Buddhist Foundation. Moreover, she involves herself in the project Modern Heroes, which encourages people to think and act beyond personal goals. She is married and has a son.

THE FOLLOWING BOOKS HAVE HAD A MAJOR INFLUENCE ON MIRIAM'S LIFE:

Healing with Qualities, Manuel Schoch
Warrior of the Light, Paulo Coelho
The Great Seal: Limitless Space and Joy, Lama Ole Nydahl
The Power of Now, Eckhart Tolle

MIRIAM
FEIST

I'm convinced that everyone creates their own experiences through actions, speech, and thoughts. This view offers immense freedom—I'm responsible for my own life. I can take it into my own hands, use each moment for my own development. With this trust in one's inherent qualities, life gets round, exciting, joyful. Consequently, it becomes natural to be interested in what is happening in the world, in the development and joy of others and our future, which we determine and form through our actions all the time. Thus we can act in a meaningful, foresightful way for the best in others.

Who Is Barbara Fields?

Barbara Fields is the executive director for the Association for Global New Thought, and cofounder/project director of the Gandhi King Season for Nonviolence. She holds many other executive positions, and she has won countless awards, including: Religious Science International's first Peace Award in 2003; the Visionary Award from the Center for New Television; and the Peace Museum's Community Peacemaker Award in the area of Diplomacy. She sits on the boards of EarthAction and the Foundation for Conscious Evolution, and she is the cofounder of the Earth Network, a nonprofit alternative television organization dedicated to the environment, social action, and the human spirit. www.agnt.org

BOOKS THAT HAVE INSPIRED BARBARA:

I and Thou, Martin Buber
Gitanjali, Rabindranath Tagore
Ethics for the New Millennium, H. H. the Dalai Lama
Turbulent Mirror, John Briggs and F. David Peat
Synergetics, Buckminster Fuller

BARBARA
FIELDS

I am striving to express the omnipresent mystery within a spiritually motivated lifestyle guided by ancient wisdom traditions. I embody a belief that consciousness is elementally creative, reciprocates thought, and thereby shapes all manifestation. My conviction is that the community of all life is sacred; our collective practices of meditation and prayerful intention promote a worldview of reverence and service toward humanity and planet Earth. Global healing is slowly (but surely) emerging through personal transformation; enlightened citizen leadership; community building; interfaith, intercultural, and interdisciplinary celebration; and compassionate activism. There is nothing here but our choices.

Who Is Ann Finlayson?

Having studied Welsh and Scottish forests for five years as a postgraduate and researcher, Ann found a niche in teaching about the environment as a Countryside Ranger in Scotland. Then for sixteen years, she traveled around the world (Papua New Guinea, Australia, and Canada) teaching, and latterly training teachers and museum and park interpreters—even white-water rafters! She also began her long interest in facilitation and participatory approaches. On returning to the UK in 2000, Ann began work at World Wildlife Fund (WWF) UK and became the head of education first, and then of social change, until early 2007. In 2005 Ann was awarded a public appointment as education commissioner for the Sustainable Development Commission, which has meant talking with many people about her vision and how to achieve it! www.sd-commission.org.uk

BOOKS THAT HAVE INSPIRED ANN:

Topophilia, Yi-fu Tuan

Multiple Intelligences, Howard Gardner

Control Theory in the Classroom, William Glasser

Facilitator's Guide to Participatory Decision-Making, Sam Kaner

Green History, Derek Wall

Education for Sustainability, John Huckle and Stephen Sterling

Oscar and Lucinda, Peter Carey

The Cultural Creatives, Paul Ray and Sherry Ruth Anderson

ANN
FINLAYSON

My vision? That we will be able to understand how to live within environmental limits and then have the confidence and abilities to do just that.

Fundamentally, then, it is about two things—learning and change.

We don't yet know how to live within environmental limits. We will have to learn, reflect, and test new ideas. There is no single solution or best practice yet. This means changing the way we think about education and learning. Then, because doing this often feels impossible, we need to find strength and support from each other to take this difficult task on. I know we can do it.

Who Is Mark A. Finser?

Mark A. Finser is chair of the RSF Social Finance Board. RSF provides innovative investing, lending, and philanthropic services to catalyze the growth of organizations creating a more sustainable future. Mark grew RSF's assets from six thousand dollars in 1984 to one hundred twenty million dollars today. In 2007 he transitioned from CEO to chair of the board. In this role, he brings even greater attention to the emerging social finance arena as he travels, in the United States and internationally. In addition, Mark founded and leads a sustainable venture fund called TBL Capital. Mark's interests include biodynamic agriculture, integrative medicine, and meditation. www.rsfsocialfinance.org, www.tblcapital.com

SOME OF MARK'S FAVORITE BOOKS:

Waking, Matthew Sanford

Money Can Heal, Siegfried Finser

Eco-Economy, Lester Brown

Blessed Unrest, Paul Hawken

How to Know Higher Worlds, Rudolf Steiner

MARK A.
FINSER

The twenty-first century stands at a threshold. Our civilization can either leave the Earth as a tomb (death of all that has come before) or a womb (life for birthing the new) for incubating a culture based on fundamentally new insights pertaining to how the Earth and humanity can transcend to a higher vibrational frequency of understanding, cooperation, and compassion. We have all the tools and ingredients—now it is up to us. I see a future where we will know, down to every cell in our social and physical bodies, that we are a multiplicity of one and that our necessary but now outdated ways of dividing science, art, and religion have led us to this current condition. Only by giving autonomy in equal emphasis to culture, human rights, and economies can our civilization thrive. Thrive by new forms of association—association with each other, the Earth, and the divine. May it be so—Oh, human, know yourself!

Who Is David Fontana?

David Fontana is a Fellow of the British Psychological Society and the first professor of transpersonal psychology in the UK. With two colleagues he founded the Transpersonal Psychology Section within the British Psychological Society and served as its foundation chair. A chartered psychologist, chartered counseling psychologist, former Distinguished Visiting Fellow at Cardiff University, and a PhD in psychology, he is the author of forty books translated into twenty-six languages. In addition to his academic psychology books, he has written extensively on meditations, dreams, and Eastern religions. His most recent books include *Psychology, Religion, and Spirituality*, and *Is There an Afterlife?*

FIVE WORKS MOST INFLUENTIAL FOR DAVID:
Founding the Life Divine, Morwenna Donnelly
Human Personality and Its Survival of Bodily Death, Frederic Myers
Memories, Dreams, Reflections, Carl Jung
The New Testament
The Varieties of Religious Experience, William James

DAVID
FONTANA

Our lives are not lonely journeys bounded by the cradle and the grave, but part of an infinite pattern that embraces all things and offers us eternal horizons. Life is not a biological accident without ultimate meaning or purpose, but a gift to be accepted with gratitude and used as a priceless opportunity for spiritual growth and understanding. Central to this understanding is the realization that we are not the lords of creation but its servants, and that it is our sacred duty to honor all life and to protect this beautiful planet that nurtures us all.

Who Is Lynne Franks?

Lynne Franks, businesswoman, author, broadcaster, and speaker, described by the world's media as a lifestyle guru and visionary, is an acclaimed international spokesperson and adviser on the changes in today's and tomorrow's world—both for the individual as well as society at large. Her consulting experience, in both the public and private sectors, her global work with women's enterprise, and her recognized gift as a "futurist" have given her considerable insight into the way forward for modern society. She is the founder of Sustainable Enterprise and Economic Dynamics (SEED), a provider of women's learning programs on economic empowerment, sustainable business practices, and community leadership. www.lynnefranks.com

BOOKS THAT HAVE MOST INSPIRED LYNNE'S LIFE:

The Fifth Sacred Thing, Starhawk

White Goddess, Robert Graves

The Chalice and the Blade, Riane Eisler

A Woman's Worth, Marianne Williamson

Women Who Run with the Wolves, Clarissa Pinkola-Estés

LYNNE
FRANKS

I believe it is time for a grassroots global revolution to ensure a future of harmony, collaboration, and spiritual prosperity for the generations to come. I believe we can create this future by combining the ancient knowledge of indigenous peoples, the wisdom of the elders, and the courage of conscious women and men leaders together with multinationals, nation states, and NGOs. I believe we have the power through our political vote as well as our consumer vote. I believe it is through women moving into, and using, their full power alongside men that we can create a new dream. I believe that it is time for the grandmothers, the women of my generation, to encourage other women to blossom and grow into the leaders that Mother Earth is crying out for.

Who Is Jessica Fullmer?

Jessica Fullmer founded the Sustainable Business Institute (SBI), which is universally renowned for bringing together global business leaders and their organizations to initiate, implement, and communicate equitable worldwide sustainability practices. SBI has created six initiatives, including its CEO Forum on Sustainable Business, and the Seal of Sustainability™ (SOS), an award for businesses and business leaders implementing sustainable practices. The SOS encourages numerous businesses to integrate and adopt sustainable business practices throughout their organizations. Jessica has appeared on a wide number of media outlets, and she is also the founder, CEO, and president of Mo-DV, Inc. (Mobile Digital Video), a premier technology provider of software for secure digital content on mobile devices. Her vision is to transform quality of life through disseminating positive, educational, and entertaining information to billions of mobile users. www.sustainablebusiness.org

BOOKS THAT HAVE INSPIRED JESSICA:

Beyond Culture, Edward T. Hall

Profound Knowledge, W. Edwards Deming

On Dialogue, David Bohm

The Limits of Thought, Jiddu Krishnamurti

The Prophet, Kahlil Gibran

JESSICA
FULLMER

The condition of our world is nothing more than a representation of our collective actions and states of mind. As such, it will always reveal the choices we've made to respect or annihilate life on our planet.

Since we all leave a footprint on this planet as we step through each day, the challenge is to make conscious choices, moment to moment, in our personal lives. Only then can we hope to ensure the sustainability of all the natural systems and life on the planet. It is impossible to improve something outside ourselves if we have not made similar changes internally. A tool to make informed choices can be the Seal of Sustainability™, created to provide hope by serving as a guide for people to purchase from businesses that are using sustainable business practices.

Who Is Howard Gardner?

Howard Gardner is an American psychologist who is based at Harvard University. The author of over twenty books translated into twenty-seven languages, and several hundred articles, Gardner is best known in educational circles for his theory of multiple intelligences, a critique of the notion that there exists but a single human intelligence that can be assessed by standard psychometric instruments. Building on his studies of intelligence, Gardner has also authored *Leading Minds, Changing Minds,* and *Extraordinary Minds.* www.howardgardner.com, www.goodworkproject.org, www.goodworktoolkit.org

INFLUENTIAL BOOKS CHOSEN BY HOWARD:

The Process of Education, Jerome Bruner

Middlemarch, George Eliot

Gandhi's Truth, Erik Erikson

Excellence, John Gardner

Exit, Voice, and Loyalty, Albert Hirschman

HOWARD
GARDNER

We do not lack the so-called "best and the brightest"—we need more individuals who do the right thing as persons, as workers, and as citizens. Good persons treat others with kindness and empathy—they exemplify the Golden Rule. Good workers are excellent technically, personally engaged in their work, and carry out their responsibilities in an ethical way. Good citizens know the laws and regulations, participate actively in the civic arena, and support policies and actions that promote the wider good. What gives me hope is that as individuals, and as groups large and small, we have the power and the agency to bring about a better world.

Who Is Zerbanoo Gifford?

Zerbanoo Gifford was named the 2006 International Woman of the Year for her humanitarian work. She holds the Nehru Centenary Award for her international work championing the cause of women and children and was also honored with the Freedom of the City of Lincoln, Nebraska, for her work against modern slavery and racism. Zerbanoo is the founder of the ASHA Foundation and the ASHA Centre for Peace and Understanding. She has written numerous books, including *Confessions of a Serial Womaniser, Secrets of the World's Inspirational Women, Dadabhai Naoroji: Britain's First Asian M.P.,* and her bestseller *The Golden Thread: Asian Experiences of Post-Raj Britain.* www.zerbanoogifford.org, www.asha-foundation.org.

FIVE BOOKS, SONGS, AND FILMS THAT HAVE INSPIRED ZERBANOO:
Bhagavad Gita
Middlemarch, George Eliot
Thomas Clarkson and the Campaign against Slavery, Zerbanoo Gifford
"My Sweet Lord," sung by George Harrison
"O Paalanhaare," from the film *Lagaan*

ZERBANOO
GIFFORD

Every summer I returned to India to stay with my beloved Bapai (paternal grand-mother) in Poona, where I would see children begging on the streets. Bapai would tell me how lucky I was to be a little girl growing up in London; she told me never to forget that I had a responsibility to help people less fortunate. On my seventh birthday, I chose to act upon her advice: I made little flags, which I sold on the street outside our family hotel in London. I made a pound, which I sent to the Prime Minister of India, Pandit Nehru. A few weeks later I received a letter back from him, thanking me and saying that "if every girl sent one pound for the poor children of Poona the problem of poverty would be on the way to being solved." As important, if every child was encouraged to express their innate goodness the way I was then—we would live in much kinder world.

Who Is Nicola Giuggioli?

Nicola Giuggioli is the founder of Eco Age Ltd. Nicola studied economics and business at the University of Rome but soon realized that if he wanted to live in a sustainable world, banking was not his future career. After earning a master's in sustainable economy and undertaking research into sustainable and environmentally conscious design and living solutions, Nicola concluded that it was almost impossible for consumers to see, touch, and evaluate different technological solutions readily available on the market. There was no one "store" in which an interested consumer could go, buy the product, and seek consultation on its complexities. And so Eco Age was born. In addition to his duties as the CEO of Eco Age, Nicola is working on several sustainable projects across Europe. www.eco-age.com

NICOLA
GIUGGIOLI

The year just gone has seen our nightmares come true, our strength tested. It's incumbent that we find more sustainable models, systems, and economies. I'm not only speaking about the climate issue. Its a social issue. A political issue. And at root, it's a matter of survival. Global warming, social division, and financial meltdown are all the result of single decisions made by individuals. I am twenty-eight years old. These decisions were taken by those much older than I am. Yet tragically, my generation will inherit the mess, wars, poisoned air and seas, the fallen banks, poverty and hatred. We are born with enemies ready made due to our parent's actions, and we will have to change the future. But, I see enormous and exciting challenges ahead, and we will have a say in our children's future. This is not a utopian dream. I want future generations to remember a movement of ordinary people (not visionaries) who gathered together to turn a seemingly hopeless situation into the roots of a new start!

Who Is Philip Golabuk?

Philip Golabuk was born in New York City and attended the University of Florida, where he worked closely with Dr. James Millikan and the late Dr. Tom Hanna. He holds undergraduate and graduate degrees in philosophy with special studies in metaphysics, phenomenology, religious philosophy, and theory of knowledge. Philip taught philosophy at the college level and as part of special outreach programs to inmates in jail and prison, and he is the author of several nonfiction books published in the United States and overseas. Fiction titles include *Hounding for Skipwaves* and *Dreams of the Chameleon*, available through Amazon.com. Philip is also the founder of the Field Center and the Moira Project. www.golabuk.com

FIVE WORKS THAT HAVE SHAPED PHILIP'S VISION:
One Hundred Years of Solitude, Gabriel García Márquez
Letters to a Young Poet, Rainer Maria Rilke
Selected Dialogues of Plato, translated by Benjamin Jowett
The Critique of Pure Reason, Immanuel Kant
The Will to Believe, William James

PHILIP
GOLABUK

I know how daunting it can all seem. Five minutes of the so-called "news" is enough to depress anyone. But in the crossfire of the headlines, at this dark hour, with even scientific predictions of doomsday and self-annihilation, a quiet and heartening light persists. The planet keeps turning, air remains breathable, and children still come into the world radiant with innocence and eager to learn and discover and take their place in the great adventure. All natural evidence demonstrates that, despite everything, life still believes in us. Perhaps we ought to trust it, and start believing in each other.

Who Is Zac Goldsmith?

Zac Goldsmith has been the director and editor of *The Ecologist* magazine for ten years. In 2005 he was invited by the UK's Conservative Party to help steer a radical review of the party's approach to the environmental crisis. The Quality of Life Policy Group delivered its recommendations on a wide range of policy issues in July 2007. In between his work with *The Ecologist* and the Conservative Party, Zac raises funds for groups around the world dealing with issues ranging from agriculture and energy to climate change and trade.

In 2003 Zac was the recipient of the Beacon Prize for Young Philanthropist of the Year. In 2004 he received the Global Green Award for International Environmental Leadership.

FIVE BOOKS THAT HAVE INSPIRED ZAC:
Another Turn of the Crank, Wendell Berry
The Way, Edward Goldsmith
1984, George Orwell
Ancient Futures, Helena Norberg-Hodge
The Count of Monte Cristo, Alexandre Dumas

ZAC
GOLDSMITH

Restoring balance to the world is a gigantic, but unavoidable, task. We face crisis on virtually every level. But each and every step we need to take is already being taken by someone, somewhere. In energy, buildings, waste, food, and farming, there are already examples of genuine best practice. That's the best possible news. It shows what can be done, and allows us the confidence of knowing what's already possible. If we are to shift from our wasteful and polluting global economy to a cleaner, more localized alternative, we need to transform today's best practice into the norm tomorrow. For people and the planet, there's only upside.

Who Is Jane Goodall?

Jane Goodall, PhD, DBE, one of the world's most famous scientists, is known for her landmark study of chimpanzees in Gombe National Park, Tanzania. Today Dr. Goodall devotes virtually all her time to advocating on behalf of chimpanzees and the environment, traveling over three hundred days a year. She is also a humanitarian and the founder of the Jane Goodall Institute and its global youth program, Roots & Shoots. In 2002 UN Secretary-General Kofi Annan appointed Dr. Goodall to serve as a United Nations Messenger of Peace, and in 2007 she was reappointed by Secretary-General Ban Ki-moon. www.janegoodall.org, www.rootsandshoots.org

FIVE BOOKS THAT IMPACTED JANE'S LIFE:
The Story of Doctor Dolittle, Hugh Lofting
Tarzan Lord of the Jungle, Edgar Rice Burroughs
Animal Liberation, Peter Singer
Silent Spring, Rachel Carson
Man's Search for Meaning, Viktor Frankl

JANE
GOODALL

So many problems: habitat destruction, poverty, pollution, population growth, over consumption, global climate change, ignorance, cruelty, hate, war. People feel helpless and so do nothing.

We have extraordinary brains, yet we are destroying our planet. We ask how major decisions will affect the next shareholders' meeting, disregarding the fate of unborn generations. There is, it seems, a disconnect between the clever brain and compassionate heart. We must become whole again.

We must realize that each of us makes a difference, every single day. We must buy ethical products, support socially and environmentally conscious politicians, walk our talk. Together we can change the world.

Who Is Miriam Greenspan?

Miriam Greenspan, MEd, LMHC, is an internationally known psychotherapist, writer, and workshop leader. She is a pioneer in women's psychology and feminist therapy, and her first book, *A New Approach to Women and Therapy,* helped define the field. For two decades, her work has been focused on a groundbreaking model of emotional alchemy and emotional ecology. Challenging current trends that devalue "negative" emotions, her more hopeful view is that in honoring our grief, fear, and despair, we are initiated into a profound healing/transformational process for ourselves and the world. *Healing Through the Dark Emotions: The Wisdom of Grief, Fear, and Despair* won the 2004 Nautilus Award in psychology/self-help for "books that make a contribution to conscious living and positive social change." Her work has been praised by Dr. Christiane Northrup, Harold Kushner, Harriet Lerner, Mary Pipher, and Joanna Macy, among others, and has been featured in many magazines, including *Spirituality & Health, Body + Soul, Shambhala Sun,* and *The Sun.* www.miriamgreenspan.com

FIVE BOOKS THAT HAVE MOST INSPIRED MIRIAM:
Shakti Woman, Vicki Noble
A Chorus of Stones, Susan Griffin
Despair and Personal Power in the Nuclear Age, Joanna Macy
Women and Madness, Phyllis Chesler
Meditation in Action, Chögyam Trungpa

MIRIAM
GREENSPAN

We live in a time of transition in which the basic assumptions, institutions, and practices of patriarchy are both breaking down and struggling for continued power. Global threat, disintegration, and chaos are, in this period, harbingers of the reemergence of the Sacred Feminine as the Dark Goddess. The long-devalued gifts of the Mother—bodily-emotional-intuitive intelligence, empathy, compassion, patience, altruism, wisdom, and fierce protection of life—are most needed now, in global proportions, for the sake of all beings and the preservation of the Earth. The current flowering of chthonic Earth consciousness is our best hope for creative transformation through our collective dark night to a healthier, saner, more balanced world.

Who Is Sylvia Greinig?

Sylvia Greinig has spent thirty-seven years creating successful learning environments for children, firstly as principal of the Catterick Garrison Prep School, then as principal of Abbey School in Torquay, Devon, UK, and as both a national curriculum moderator and Ofsted inspector. Whilst at Exeter University, UK, Sylvia became greatly influenced by the work of world-renowned philosopher Matthew Lipman and his philosophy for children, finally working with him in New Jersey in 1996. Sylvia is married, has two daughters, and is a pillar of her local community, where she is involved with several business community projects, including the Whitley Wildlife Conservation Trust. www.abbeyschool.co.uk

FIVE BOOKS THAT HAVE HELPED TO SHAPE SYLVIA'S LIFE:
Changing Children's Minds, Howard Sharron
Intelligence Reframed, Howard Gardner
Jonathan Livingston Seagull, Richard Bach
The Diary of a Nobody, George & Weedon Grossmith
Birds of Britain and Ireland, John Googers

SYLVIA
GREINIG

Unconditional Love vs. Indifference.

Children deserve unconditional love. When they make errors of judgment, as we all do from time to time, they need to know that we may not like what they have done, but we still love them. It is not a denial of love to acknowledge poor behavior. The lie or exaggeration should be corrected; the spiteful deed or unkind word must be remedied. Ignoring such lapses has nothing to do with love. It simply rewards poor behavior and displays our indifference.

Who Is Bradley Trevor Greive?

After starting out as a paratroop platoon commander, Bradley Trevor Greive (BTG) has subsequently written numerous international bestsellers, including *The Blue Day Book* and *Priceless: The Vanishing Beauty of a Fragile Planet*. Passionate about wildlife and wild places, BTG is currently governor of the Taronga Foundation in Australia, honorary international conservation ambassador for the Fort Worth Zoo in the United States, a patron of Painted Dog Conservation Inc. in Australia/Africa, and life benefactor of the Durrell Wildlife Conservation Trust in the United Kingdom. He is also chairman of the Taronga Foundation Poetry Prize, a proud supporter of the Australian Youth Orchestra, and an ambassador for the Dymocks Literacy Foundation. www.btgstudios.com

FIVE OF BRADLEY'S FAVORITE BOOKS:

My Family and Other Animals, Gerald Durrell
A Book of Luminous Things, Czeslaw Milosz
Siddhartha, Hermann Hesse
Genius, James Gleick
Independent People, Halldór Laxness

SOMEBODY WHO DEEPLY INSPIRED BRADLEY'S LIFE:

Billy Collins, the former U.S. Poet Laureate, whose light yet exquisite touch with words helped Bradley to fall in love with poetry all over again. Bradley says that Collins's book, *Taking Off Emily Dickinson's Clothes* is probably the best place to begin, being that it is an anthology containing poems from a number of his books.

BRADLEY
TREVOR
GREIVE

There is no obstacle in this life that will not yield to compassion, creativity, and courage.

Who Is John Hagelin?

John Hagelin, PhD, is a world-renowned quantum physicist, educator, and public policy expert, and a leading proponent of peace. He has conducted groundbreaking research at the European Center for Particle Physics (CERN) and the Stanford Linear Accelerator Center (SLAC), and his many scientific contributions include some of the most cited references in the physical sciences. He is responsible for the development of a highly successful grand unified field theory based on the superstring, and he has pioneered the use of unified field–based *technologies* derived from the ancient Vedic science of consciousness to reduce crime, violence, terrorism, and war and to promote peace throughout society. In recognition of his outstanding achievements, Dr. Hagelin was named winner of the prestigious Kilby Award, which recognizes scientists who have made "major contributions to society through their applied research in the fields of science and technology." The award recognized Dr. Hagelin as "a scientist in the tradition of Einstein, Jeans, Bohr and Eddington." www.hagelin.org

BOOKS THAT HAVE INFLUENCED JOHN'S LIFE AND WORK:
The Science of Being and Art of Living, Maharishi Mahesh Yogi
Maharishi Mahesh Yogi on the Bhagavad Gita:
   A New Translation and Commentary
Human Physiology, Tony Nader
The Elegant Universe, Brian Greene
The Owl and the Pussycat, Edward Lear and Anne Mortimer

JOHN
HAGELIN

Recent breakthroughs in quantum physics have revealed the *unified field*, the field of universal intelligence at the basis of mind and matter. We must now harness this cutting-edge knowledge to create a peaceful, harmonious, enlightened world. Through Transcendental Meditation, we can directly access and experience this unified field as pure consciousness—a fourth major state of consciousness distinct from waking, dreaming, and sleeping. This fundamental experience develops full human potential—total brain functioning—and simultaneously creates long-range "field effects" of consciousness that defuse acute societal stress and conflict. The inevitable outcome will be enlightenment for the individual and lasting peace on Earth.

Who Is Anna Halprin?

James Roose-Evans, author of *Experimental Theatre,* called Anna Halprin one of the most important theater artists of the twentieth century. The Dance Heritage Coalition has named Anna Halprin one of America's Irreplaceable Dance Treasures.

Anna is considered a pioneer in using dance as a healing art. She has cultivated a process by which everyone can develop their natural sense of creativity through movement.

She is the author of *Movement Ritual, Moving Toward Life: Five Decades of Transformational Dance,* and *Returning to Health with Dance, Movement and Imagery.* Her films include *Returning Home,* a stunning dance documentation of her connection to nature. At eighty-nine, Anna continues to perform and teach with fervor, leading workshops and large group rituals worldwide. www.annahalprin.org

FIVE BOOKS THAT IMPACTED ANNA'S LIFE:

The RSVP Cycles, Lawrence Halprin

Cancer as a Turning Point, Lawrence Leshan, PhD

Technicians of the Sacred, edited with commentary by Jerome Rothenberg

Art and Life, Udo Kultermann

The Illuminated Rumi, translated with commentary by Coleman Barks

ANNA
HALPRIN

There may be a future where more of us will call ourselves artists and work together to make art concerned with the primary issues of life. There may be a future where art is once again honored for its power to inspire, teach, transform, and heal. There may be a future in which all people dance together, when the circle is open enough for both grandparents and children, people of any color or culture or spiritual practice. There may be a future when we will ask to join the four-legged and winged creatures and the creepy-crawlies, the mountains, oceans, sun and moon, the rainforests, instead of asking them to join us. There may be a future that is all of this, or there may be no future at all.

Who Is Stuart Hameroff?

Stuart Hameroff, MD, is a clinical anesthesiologist, professor of anesthesiology and psychology, and director of the Center for Consciousness Studies at the University of Arizona in Tucson. Beginning in the early 1970s, Hameroff has studied biomolecular mechanisms underlying consciousness, actions of anesthetic gases, and information processing in cytoskeletal microtubules inside living cells. In 1994 Hameroff teamed with British physicist Sir Roger Penrose in the controversial Orch-OR theory of consciousness, based on quantum computations in microtubules inside neurons. Hameroff has appeared in the films *What the Bleep Do We Know?!* and *Secrets of the Soul,* and has coauthored another film, *Mindville.* www.quantumconsciousness.org

BOOKS AND MUSICAL GROUPS THAT HAVE INFLUENCED STUART:
Introduction to a Sub-Molecular Biology, Albert Szent-Györgyi
Languages of the Brain, Karl Pribram
The Emperor's New Mind, Roger Penrose
The Beatles
Bob Dylan

STUART
HAMEROFF

Brain mechanisms underlying consciousness will be found not only in neuronal firings and synaptic transmissions, but also in quantum computations in biomolecular structures inside neurons, coupled to quantum ripples in the irreducible level of the universe—fundamental spacetime geometry. At this level, Planck scale geometry (twenty-five orders of magnitude smaller than atoms) is a hologram, embedding protoconscious and Platonic values (suggested by Penrose, 1989). Non-local quantum entanglement implies consciousness involves:

1. Interconnectedness among living beings and the universe
2. Cosmic intelligence affecting conscious choices and perceptions
3. Possible existence of consciousness after death

Quantum consciousness will scientifically validate secular spirituality.

Who Is Fiona Harrold?

Born in Northern Ireland, and growing up during the height of the sectarian troubles, Fiona studied English literature and politics at the University of Ulster. She spent the early 1980s as a political activist, campaigning at Greenham Common nuclear weapons base, writing for a community newspaper, and supporting the 1984 miners' strike. She set up the London College of Massage, selling it in 1996. Now a popular motivational speaker, Fiona currently teaches coaching skills to officers in UK prisons, works with excluded teenagers in Belfast, and runs programs for the unemployed in ex-mining communities across the UK. In 2005 she represented the Green Party at the general election. Her books include *Be Your Own Life Coach, The 10-Minute Life Coach,* and *The 7 Rules of Success.* www.fionaharrold.com

FIVE BOOKS THAT INSPIRED FIONA:

You Can Heal Your Life, Louise L. Hay
All Men Are Brothers, Mahatma Gandhi
Middlemarch, George Eliot
The Power of Positive Thinking, Norman Vincent Peale
Conversations with God, Neale Donald Walsch

FIONA
HARROLD

We are more affluent than any other generation, yet less content. Perhaps we needed to experience this to know it. The challenge for all of us is to give our lives a sense of purpose and express our fullest potential in the process. We all have a calling, to contribute to something bigger than ourselves, something that brings out our talent and passion. We no longer have to travel to a third world to find a mission. The opportunity to play our part can be on our doorstep. The reward is a depth of fulfillment no amount of money can buy. And we also seem to be grasping that life is short. The more we contribute, the more we get out of life.

Who Is Richard Heinberg?

Richard Heinberg is the author of eight books, including *The Party's Over: Oil, War and the Fate of Industrial Societies*; *Powerdown: Options and Actions for a Post-Carbon World*; *The Oil Depletion Protocol*; and *Peak Everything*. He is a Senior Fellow at the Post Carbon Institute and is widely regarded as one of the world's foremost peak oil educators. He writes a regular column for *The Ecologist* magazine and has authored scores of essays and articles that have appeared in such journals as *The American Prospect, Public Policy Research, The Quarterly Review, Resurgence, The European Business Review, Earth Island Journal, Yes!, Pacific Ecologist,* and *Wild Matters* and on Web sites such as Alternet.org, EnergyBulletin.net, GlobalPublicMedia.com, ProjectCensored.com, and Counterpunch.com. www.richardheinberg.com

FIVE BOOKS THAT INSPIRED RICHARD TO SEARCH MORE DEEPLY:
Overshoot, William R. Catton, Jr.
Cultural Materialism, Marvin Harris
Myth of the Machine, Lewis Mumford
A Prosperous Way Down, Howard T. Odum and Elisabeth C. Odum
The Collapse of Complex Societies, Joseph Tainter

RICHARD
HEINBERG

When I was younger, I envisioned a utopian future for humanity. Now I look at the sobering ecological deficit we are running up as a species—nearly seven billion of us, our economies based on consuming both nonrenewable resources like oil and coal, and also renewable ones, though at rates that overwhelm Earth's abilities to replenish them—and I hope merely that we can navigate the inevitable societal contraction in a way that preserves both habitat for other species and the best of what we have achieved culturally. A sustainable way of life will be far more satisfying; the transition's the trick.

Who Is F. Xavier Helgesen?

F. Xavier Helgesen cofounded Better World Books at the age of twenty-three. Better World Books, a B Corporation that sells books online to fund literacy, has raised over seven million dollars for worldwide literacy and is setting a new standard for conscious capitalism. ww.betterworldbooks.com

FIVE BOOKS THAT INSPIRED XAVIER:

Energy and Equity, Ivan Illich

Eco Barons, Edward Humes

Natural Capitalism, Paul Hawken, L. Hunter Lovins, and Amory Lovins

The Ecology of Commerce, Paul Hawken

Earth from Above, Yann Arthus-Bertrand

F. XAVIER
HELGESEN

My vision is Gross Domestic Product thrown out the window as a measure of progress. As long as GDP dominates the economic discussion, our world will suffer. Think about it for a moment. . . . A mother leaves her job to stay home and raise a family: GDP goes down. Brazil cuts down its rainforests to plant soybeans: GDP skyrockets. A commuter dumps his car for a bike: GDP takes a dive. In all cases, GDP moves opposite to society and ecology. In my vision, we'll measure our natural capital accurately and start managing our ecological and social balance sheets.

Who Is Hazel Henderson?

Hazel Henderson is a futurist and an economic iconoclast. In recent years she has worked in television, and she is the author of several books, including *Building a Win-Win World, Beyond Globalization, Planetary Citizenship* (with Daisaku Ikeda), and *Ethical Markets: Growing the Green Economy*. In 2007 Henderson started EthicalMarkets.tv to showcase video of people and organizations around the world with socially responsible endeavors. Practicing what she preaches, Henderson sought out highly efficient technology to stream the video, MIPBSCast, which uses significantly less energy than most other video platforms. Henderson is now a television producer for the public television series Ethical Markets. www.hazelhenderson.com, www.ethicalmarkets.com, www.calvert-henderson.com

HAZEL
HENDERSON

I expect that Western and all other economies will have corrected their Gross National Product and other indicators to measure real wealth, progress, and quality of life. As these changes, already underway, proceed, better public and private decision-making will steer societies toward healthy goals: peace, cooperation, social justice, environmental protection, citizen participation in democracies, and sustainable paths toward human development. Numerous global surveys in sixty countries, north, south, east, and west, find large majorities of citizens supporting these goals. Civic society is becoming the world's newest superpower. Linked with democratized media, we can make these goals a reality in this century.

Who Are Kathlyn and Gay Hendricks?

Kathlyn and Gay Hendricks are major contributors to the fields of conscious relationships and body-mind vibrance. They are the authors of more than twenty books, including such bestsellers as *Conscious Loving, Five Wishes, The Corporate Mystic,* and *Conscious Living.* During the past thirty years they have appeared on hundreds of radio and television shows, including *Oprah,* CNN, CNBC, and CBS's *48 Hours.*

Gay Hendricks received his PhD in counseling psychology from Stanford in 1974. Kathlyn Hendricks received her doctorate from the Institute of Transpersonal Psychology in 1982. In 1989 they founded the Hendricks Institute, which offers seminars annually in North America, Asia, and Europe. Their nonprofit organization, the Foundation for Conscious Living, funds research, films, and scholarships in the area of conscious relationships and body-mind vibrance. They are also the cofounders, with Stephen Simon, of the Spiritual Cinema Circle.

The Hendricks live in Ojai, California. www.hendricks.com

KATHLYN
AND GAY
HENDRICKS

**A GLOBAL REVOLUTION: CHANGING HOW WE COMMUNICATE
IN LOVE, WORK, AND POLITICS**

Your Invitation

   We'd like to invite you to join us in a special kind of revolution—one in which everybody wins and nobody gets hurt. For many years we have had the privilege and joy of helping people change their lives and their relationships by learning how to use four communication tools skillfully. We originally discovered the power of those tools thirty years ago, by experimenting in our own relationship with ways to keep the flow of intimacy going strong between us. The tools work, and we've been rewarded with more love, harmony, and creativity than we ever imagined possible.

   Here are the positive actions that create genuine miracles in living and loving. You can expect miraculous transformation when you do four things:

1. Speak honestly (instead of concealing the truth)
2. Take healthy responsibility (instead of blaming others)
3. Express appreciation (instead of expressing chronic criticism)
4. Wonder (instead of worrying) about the challenges you face

At the same time that we've been living on this steady diet of miracles in our own life and work, we have been growing increasingly frustrated with the political world we live in. Specifically, the thing that most frustrates us is the unwillingness of politicians to use those four miracle-tools. In fact, not only do they refuse to use them, they expend great energy practicing the exact opposite tactics: lying, blaming, belittling others, and self-righteous proclaiming.

Determining the Future

We would like your support on a global initiative that will bring the solution to these problems to the attention of political leaders everywhere. An initiative is defined as the "first step in a process that determines the future." A revolution is a "dramatic change in ideas or practice." We invite you to join the revolution and take the initiative.

First, let's bring it into being through the power of our collective imagination:

Imagine a world in which everybody tells the truth.

Imagine a world in which nobody blames and everybody takes 100 percent responsibility for creating positive solutions.

Imagine a world in which we all expand in wonder, love, and creativity every day.

Who Is Sue Holden?

Sue Holden is the chief executive of the Woodland Trust, the UK's leading woodland conservation organization. The trust is focused on creating new woodland— the UK is one of the least wooded parts of Europe—and on protecting existing woodland, especially ancient woodland, which makes up 2 percent of the land.

Ancient woodland is the UK's rainforest, home to more threatened species than any other UK wildlife habitat—and it is irreplaceable. In the past two years, the Woodland Trust has engaged over five hundred thousand people, especially children, in tree planting, and to date, almost three million trees have been planted. www.woodlandtru

SUE'S FAVORITE BOOK:

The Man Who Planted Trees, Jean Giono

SUE HOLDEN

I hope for a future where the environment is respected, completely and un-conditionally, for the benefits it provides people and for its intrinsic value. My message is that trees and forests have an incredible role to play—they are the very lifeblood of our planet. They stabilize soil, store carbon, transform our landscapes, reduce flooding, and provide one of the richest habitats for flora and fauna. They provide a sustainable material and carbon-neutral fuel. They inspire imagination and culture and learning. Sadly, forests are disappearing all over the world and climate change will put trees under enormous stress. But what really gives me hope is that, whilst solving the causes of deforestation is extremely difficult, planting more trees is extremely easy. Plant a tree now!

Who Is Patrick Holford?

Patrick Holford, BS, Dip ION, FBant, is widely regarded as Britain's bestselling author and leading spokesperson on nutrition, food, environmental, and health issues. In 1984 he founded the Institute for Optimum Nutrition (ION), a charitable and independent educational trust for the furtherance of education and research in nutrition. The institute offers degree-accredited training in nutritional therapy. In 2003 Patrick also founded the Brain Bio Centre at ION, a treatment center pioneering the Optimum Nutrition approach for mental health. He is frequently involved in government-led campaigns, and has previously attended the House of Commons, the House of Lords, and the Food Standards Agency as an expert in Optimum Nutrition. His knowledge and ability to simplify complex issues enable students to expand their understanding of vital health issues. www.patrickholford.com

WORKS THAT HAVE MOVED PATRICK:

Glass Bead Game, Hermann Hesse

Maverick!, Ricardo Semler

Adventures in Psychiatry, Dr. Abram Hoffer

Play of Consciousness, Swami Muktananda

Never Mind the Bollocks, Here's the Sex Pistols, the Sex Pistols

PATRICK
HOLFORD

We have created most twenty-first-century diseases—cancer, heart disease, diabetes, obesity, Alzheimer's—through a change in diet and lifestyle. We are literally digging our own graves with a knife and fork. We have lost a sense of connection with the Earth, food, our bodies, and ourselves. Mental health problems from Alzheimer's or depression to schizophrenia are ever increasing. The new science of Optimum Nutrition, taking into account our genetic uniqueness and treating not with drugs, but personalized diet and nutritional supplements, is the new paradigm in medicine. This is the future of medicine for an enlightened humanity.

Who Is John Holland?

John Holland is an internationally renowned psychic medium who has spent more than twenty years investigating and developing his abilities as a spirit messenger. It was after a near-fatal car accident in his early thirties that his long-suppressed skills were released. John regularly lectures on both the East and West coasts, and his public demonstrations provide his audience with a unique glimpse into the fascinating subject of mediumship, which he discusses in his uniquely humorous style, combined with his pure intensity and compassion. John's work has been featured on TV in *Unsolved Mysteries*, and he has also been interviewed on *Extra* and the Telemundo channel. www.johnholland.com

BOOKS THAT HAVE INSPIRED JOHN:
Autobiography of a Yogi, Paramahansa Yogananda
Power of the Soul, John Holland
Many Lives, Many Masters, Brian Weiss
There Is a River, Thomas Sugrue
The Unmistakable Touch of Grace, Cheryl Richardson

JOHN
HOLLAND

All I'm asking is to be conscious of helping another. You may be saying: "But, I'm just one person. What can I do?" You can't change the world—but you can start by changing yourself. Whatever is going on in the inside will be reflected on the outside. Everything in the world is based on the inner consciousness of man. Always remember that one person (that means you) can make all the difference. You are a soul, and we're all connected, so believe and know that you do have power and you *do* matter in this collective universe.

Who Is Rob Hopkins?

Rob is a permaculture designer and teacher who lived for many years in Ireland, where he developed the first two-year permaculture course in the world at Kinsale FE College—built with cob and straw bales—and wrote and lectured widely. On his return to his native England, he initiated the Transition movement: communities across the UK and beyond who are engaging creatively with the twin challenges of peak oil and climate change. He founded Transition Town Totnes and the Transition Network, publishes www.transitionculture.org, and is the author of *The Transition Handbook: From Oil Dependency to Local Resilience*. His passions are nut trees, cob, and myrtle berries.

BOOKS THAT CHANGED ROB'S LIFE:

Permaculture, Bill Mollison and David Holmgren

Coming Back to Life, Joanna Macy and Molly Young Brown

Peak Everything, Richard Heinberg

Creating a World that Works for All, Sharif Abdullah

The Nature of Order, Christopher Alexander

ROB
HOPKINS

My vision is of a more localized, small-scale yet more abundant society developed in enough time to avoid the worst impacts of peak oil and climate change. It saw the crisis coming, applying its collective genius to rethinking basic assumptions, emerging more rooted in place, creative, skilled, time-rich, and connected to nature. In this world, local food, building materials, currencies, energy generation, and medicines have led to an economic renaissance. Our role at this time is to paint such vivid pictures of this world that our lives will feel bereft if we aren't moving, with considerable speed, toward them.

Who Is John Houghton?

John Houghton is a scientist who has held positions as professor of atmospheric physics at Oxford, chief executive of the Meteorological Office, and chairman of the Royal Commission on Environmental Pollution. He assisted in 1988 with the formation of the Intergovernmental Panel on Climate Change (IPCC), chaired or cochaired its Scientific Assessment Working Group until 2002, and was part of the delegation that received the Nobel Peace Prize awarded to the IPCC in 2007. He is currently the president of the John Ray Initiative and a trustee of the Shell Foundation. His many awards include the Japan Prize, gold medals from the Royal Astronomical Society and the Royal Meteorological Society, and honorary doctorates from a number of UK universities. His books include *Global Warming: The Complete Briefing* and *The Search for God: Can Science Help?* www.jri.org.uk

BOOKS THAT HAVE DEEPLY INFLUENCED JOHN'S LIFE:

Surprised by Joy, C. S. Lewis
Earth in the Balance, Al Gore
Rich Christians in an Age of Hunger, Ronald Sider
The Message of Creation, David Wilkinson

JOHN
HOUGHTON

My vision is for the threat of global climate change, so devastating especially to poorer countries, to bring about a sustainable and fairer world, where natural resources are valued not squandered, where rich nations share wealth and skills with poorer ones, and where the net flow of wealth is no longer from poor to rich. How can this transformation happen? I believe through bringing God into the equation (science and God are not opposed!), by humbly accepting his strength and wisdom, and by applying honest science and appropriate technology together with qualities of faith, hope, and love (thank you, St. Paul, for your inspiring triad!).

Who Is Jean Houston?

Dr. Jean Houston, scholar, philosopher, and researcher in Human Capacities, is one of the foremost visionary thinkers and doers of our time. She is one of the principal founders of the Human Potential Movement. Dr. Houston is a prolific writer and the author of twenty-six books, including *A Passion for the Possible*, *Search for the Beloved*, *A Mythic Life*, *Jump Time*, and *Manual for the Peacemaker*. A powerful and dynamic speaker, she holds conferences and seminars with social leaders, educational institutions, and business organizations worldwide. Dr. Houston has worked intensively in forty cultures in over one hundred countries and is currently broadening her work with the United Nations as a senior adviser to the United Nations Development Programme. www.jeanhouston.org

BOOKS THAT HAVE INFLUENCED AND INSPIRED JEAN'S LIFE:

A Study of History, Arnold Joseph Toynbee

A Wind in the Door, Madeleine L'Engle

Joseph and His Brethren, Thomas Mann

The Tempest, Shakespeare

Phenomenology of Spirit, G. W. F. Hegel

JEAN
HOUSTON

We are at that stage where the real work of humanity begins. This is the time and place where we partner Creation in the re-creation of ourselves, in the restoration of the biosphere, and in the assuming of a new kind of culture—what we might term a culture of kindness, where we live daily life in such a way as to be reconnected, charged, and intelligenced by the source of our reality to become liberated as to our inventiveness and very engaged in our world and our tasks. Now there is a quickening, an almost desperate sense of need for this possible human in us all to help create the possible society and the possible world, if we are to survive our own personal and planetary odyssey.

Who Is Steve Howard?

Steve Howard is the CEO of the Climate Group, which he cofounded in late 2003. He has worked on a variety of social and environmental issues from within business, NGO, and UN settings. While at the Climate Group, he has advised many world leading companies on climate change strategy and has chaired meetings with business and government leaders, including the Long Beach meeting of business leaders with Governor Arnold Schwarzenegger and Prime Minister Tony Blair. www.theclimategroup.org

BOOKS, A SONG, AND A MOVIE THAT HAVE INSPIRED STEVE'S LIFE:

Long Walk to Freedom, Nelson Mandela

I, Robot, Isaac Asimov

Animal Farm, George Orwell

"What a Wonderful World," Nat King Cole

Life Is Beautiful, director Roberto Benigni

STEVE
HOWARD

"WE'RE IN THIS TOGETHER"

"The Tragedy of the Commons" describes how herders always chose to keep a maximum number of grazing stock, despite degradation of the finite pasture. Reducing numbers to benefit overgrazed land held no gain for individual herders. This short-term attitude to individual returns over the common good has a powerful parallel with climate change. Nobody can reap the benefits of a stable climate unless we *all* reduce our greenhouse gases. Rather than suffer the Tragedy of the Atmosphere, I hope this generation will make decisions in our collective long-term interest. This will require a political shift bringing results beyond the next election, business shift producing non-polluting products that do not drain finite resources, and a cultural shift where people realize that we may all act alone, but we're still in this together.

Who Is Barbara Marx Hubbard?

Barbara Marx Hubbard is the founder of the Foundation for Conscious Evolution. A speaker, social innovator, and author of five books, Barbara is an evolutionary educator, communicating the new worldview of conscious evolution. She has established a chair in Conscious Evolution for Wisdom University. She is currently producing a film series titled *Humanity Ascending: A New Way through Together*. Her educational program Gateway to Conscious Evolution, a guided evolutionary curriculum, is reaching over one thousand people worldwide. She is assembling a Conscious Evolution Archives and Library in Santa Barbara, California, to focus on the many dimensions of her work as well as other pioneering leaders in this new field. She produced twenty-five Synergistic Convergence (SYNCON) conferences to bring opposing groups together in the light of the potential of the whole system, and is now reviving the SYNCON process. She received a first doctorate in conscious evolution from Emerson Theological Institute and has been a founding board member of many organizations, including the World Future Society and the Association for Global New Thought.

KEY BOOKS IN BARBARA'S LIFE:

Thank God for Evolution, Michael Dowd
Quantum Shift in the Global Brain, Ervin Laszlo
Nature's Magic: Synergy in Evolution and
    the Fate of Humankind, Peter Corning
The Singularity Is Near, Ray Kurzweil
The Meaning of the 21st Century, James Martin
Blessed Unrest, Paul Hawken

BARBARA
MARX
HUBBARD

We are at the threshold of the first Age of Conscious Evolution. An evolution from unconscious to conscious choice.

Our problems are awakening us to evolve more consciously or we will destroy our life-support system within the next generation. This is the greatest calling humanity has ever faced.

The Impulse of Evolution is rising up from deep within and each of us has a purpose to become more creative, expressive, and fulfil our potential.

When we say YES to that purpose, the Process of Creation intensifies within us.

Many of us are entering the ever-growing global communion of pioneering souls. We are ready to build our "Peace Room" to scan for, map, connect, and communicate what is working to heal and evolve our world beyond war.

As a universal species, we are capable of restoring our Earth, freeing ourselves from hunger, ignorance, and disease, shifting from war to conscious evolution, moving toward life ever-evolving in a universe of immeasurable dimensions.

Who Is Tim Jackson?

Tim Jackson is a professor of sustainable development and director of the ESRC Research Group on Lifestyles, Values, and Environment at the University of Surrey, England. He is also the economics commissioner on the UK Sustainable Development Commission and sits on the Environment Agency's Science Advisory Panel. His publications include *Material Concerns* and *The Earthscan Reader on Sustainable Consumption.* Aside from his environmental work, Tim is an award-winning playwright with a string of radio-writing credits for the BBC. www.surrey.ac.uk/resolve, www.sd-commission.org.uk

BOOKS THAT HAVE GREATLY IMPACTED TIM'S LIFE:

The Sacred Canopy, Peter Berger
Zen Mind, Beginner's Mind, Shunryu Suzuki
War and Peace, Leo Tolstoy
The Body Has Its Reasons, Thérèse Bertherat
The Red Queen, Matt Ridley

TIM
JACKSON

For weeks I wondered what to write here. What words could possibly capture my fragile, translucent hopes for humankind? And then last night I dreamt I found this book. Its pages were already tattered. Its words long since indecipherable. And there was no longer space for me to write down anything. It bothered me at first, of course. But then I asked myself, what really was there left to say? And I realized, with blinding clarity, absolutely nothing! Nada. Nichts. Rien. Niente. Hnyero … Nothing. The future was already here. Free at last, I woke up smiling.

Who Is Marcia Jaffe?

Marcia Jaffe is considered a global entrepreneur since her leap into creating large conferences that bring together indigenous wisdom of the Balinese with people from around the world who are ready to become more active around their personal passions. She is the founder and has been the president of the Bali Institute for Global Renewal for over five years, bringing together programs, seminars, and other gatherings focused on leadership, activism, and indigenous wisdom. More than fifteen hundred people have attended these programs, and she will soon be building an entirely new kind of conference facility in Bali that incorporates Balinese architecture, cultural collaboration, and village involvement. www.baliinstitute.org

FIVE OF MARCIA'S FAVORITE BOOKS:

Letters to a Young Poet, Rainer Maria Rilke

Poems, Mary Oliver

The Spell of the Sensuous, David Abram

When the Heart Waits, Sue Monk Kidd

Report to Greco, Nikos Kazantzakis

MARCIA
JAFFE

Life is such an extraordinarily fragile gift. We need to understand how precious our capacities and beliefs are and what they can deliver to the world. We must take ourselves really seriously and use our enormous ability to imagine and to dream. Then, we must find our passion, take that tremendous energy into the world, and do something. We are the leaders we have been waiting for. We can make a difference. It's all about believing that you have the power to create the world you want to live in.

Who Is Gerald Jampolsky?

Gerald G. Jampolsky, MD, is a graduate of Stanford Medical School and an internationally recognized authority in the fields of psychiatry, health, and education. In 1975 he established the original Center for Attitudinal Healing in Tiburon, California, where children and adults with life challenges as well as life-threatening illness find peace of mind that is transforming for them and their families. Through his work at the center, Dr. Jampolsky created the first peer support group model now used extensively worldwide. In 2005 he received one of the highest awards in medicine from the AMA for his innovative work in Attitudinal Healing. Dr. Jampolsky has published extensively and is the author of *Love Is Letting Go of Fear* and numerous other bestselling books. www.jerryjampolsky.com

**A BOOK AND A WRITING THAT HAVE DEEPLY INSPIRED
GERALD'S LIFE PATH:**
A Course in Miracles, The Foundation for Inner Peace

*What lies behind us
And what lies before us
Are tiny matters compared to
What lies within us*
—Ralph Waldo Emerson

GERALD
JAMPOLSKY

At eighty-two years of age, I am an eternal optimist and full of hope for a future that is filled with Love. Each of us has the ability to make a decision to release the past through forgiving the past and to live in the present. I am convinced that our Attitudes are everything. Our limitless imagination can take us to a new reality that is beyond our beliefs and into a sense of knowing.

Who Is Susan Jeffers?

Susan Jeffers, PhD, is considered one of the top self-help authors in the world. *The Times* (London) named Susan "The Queen of Self-Help." Her first book, *Feel the Fear and Do It Anyway*, launched her career as a bestselling author. Seventeen more books have followed, the latest being *The Feel the Fear Guide to Lasting Love.* Her books have been published in over one hundred countries and have been translated into thirty-six languages. Susan recently created a publishing company, Jeffers Press, to publish her own books and those of other inspirational writers. www.susanjeffers.com

FIVE OF SUSAN'S FAVORITE BOOKS:

Man's Search for Meaning, Viktor Frankl

Chop Wood, Carry Water, Rick Fields

We're All Doing Time, Bo Lozoff

Still Here, Ram Dass

Awakening the Buddha Within, Lama Surya Das

SUSAN
JEFFERS

It's all in your perception. If you see your tasks in life as drudgery, then they are drudgery. On the other hand, if you see them as gifts of the universe manifest through you, then your tasks are done in the spirit of love and generosity. You step out of your ordinary life and make it extraordinary. Little by little, you realize that your life truly makes a difference and you are filled with a wondrous sense of gratitude and abundant flow. A heavenly feeling, indeed! Yes, it's all in your perception.

Who Is Van Jones?

Van Jones was the special adviser for Green Jobs, Enterprise, and Innovation at the White House Council on Environmental Quality (CEQ) until he was forced to resign in September 2009. He is an environmental advocate, a civil rights activist and attorney, and an author. Formerly based in Oakland, California, Jones is the founder of Green for All, a national NGO dedicated to building an inclusive green economy strong enough to lift people out of poverty. His first book, *The Green Collar Economy*, was a *New York Times* bestseller. Jones also founded the Ella Baker Center for Human Rights, a California NGO working for alternatives to violence and incarceration. In 2008 *Time* magazine named Jones one of its Environmental Heroes. *Fast Company* called him one of the 12 Most Creative Minds of 2008. Jones lives in the D.C. area with his wife and two young sons. www.vanjones.net, www.greenforall.org

INDIVIDUALS AND WORKS THAT HAVE INSPIRED VAN'S LIFE AND WORK:

The Making of Black Revolutionaries, James Forman
The Fire Next Time, James Baldwin
No Fist Is Big Enough to Hide the Sky, Basil Davidson
Amilcar Cabral
Patrick Chabal
Bob Marley

VAN
JONES

The green economy can do more than create business opportunities for the rich—it can also create job opportunities for the poor. While curbing global warming and oil dependence, we can also create good jobs, safer streets, and healthier communities. We dream of seeing kids who are now fodder for the prisons instead creating zero-pollution products, healing the land, and harvesting the sun. Some will call this unrealistic and advise us to keep our dreams small. But that cynicism is the problem in our country, not the solution. We dream of a multiethnic, grassroots movement transforming urban America by creating jobs, reducing violence, and honoring the Earth. We see it as the chief moral obligation in the twenty-first century: to build a green economy strong enough to lift people out of poverty.

Who Is Tony Juniper?

Tony Juniper is the director of Friends of the Earth and vice chair of Friends of the Earth International. His environmental work spans more than twenty years and ranges from activities with primary school children on local conservation projects to helping the global campaign to highlight the impacts of world trade policy on the environment. He has been a leading figure in many of the main environmental campaigns of recent times, including the anti-road building protests of the 1990s and the mobilization against GM crops and foods. His present focus is climate change. In addition to running Friends of the Earth, and his lobbying and public awareness work, he writes and comments on environmental issues. Tony is a naturalist, an ornithologist, and a recognized expert on parrots. He is the coauthor of the award-winning *Parrots: A Guide to the Parrots of the World* and of the widely acclaimed *Spix's Macaw: The Race to Save the World's Rarest Bird*. He is also the author of *How Many Lightbulbs Does It Take to Change a Planet?: 95 Ways to Save Planet Earth*. www.tonyjuniper.com

FIVE BOOKS THAT HAVE DEEPLY INSPIRED TONY:

When Corporations Rule the World, David Korten
Life on Earth, David Attenborough
Biodiversity, E. O. Wilson
Six Degrees, Mark Lynas
First Light, Geoffrey Wellum

TONY
JUNIPER

The creativity and brilliance of humanity could so easily be harnessed to create paradise. We already know how to sustainably farm, use low carbon energy technologies, conserve nature, and live efficiently. If we turned our attention to solving the twin crises of environmental degradation and deepening inequality, then we could all live in comfort and feel secure. The missing ingredients are not technological; pretty much all we need for everyone's needs to be met sustainably is already invented. The challenge is economic and political. A different economic system that values the Earth is what's required. The intellectual work for this is largely done: now we need leadership and inspiration to give it life. A new approach to development needs to be built on cooperation more than competition, and geared toward well-being rather than crude growth.

Who Is Georgia Kelly?

Georgia Kelly is the founder and executive director of Praxis Peace Institute in Sonoma, California. She has created education programs and conferences focused on peace building, conflict transformation, democratic participation, and the transformation of culture. She is also a harpist, composer, and recording artist. www.praxispeace.org

BOOKS THAT HAVE EDUCATED AND INSPIRED GEORGIA:

Eros and Civilization, Herbert Marcuse

Faces of the Enemy, Sam Keen

Being Peace, Thich Nhat Hanh

Sacred Pleasure, Riane Eisler

The Guru Papers, Diana Alstad and Joel Kramer

The Creation of Patriarchy, Gerda Lerner

GEORGIA
KELLY

We have reached a cultural crisis, a breakdown of old forms that requires a different approach from the ones learned in the dominator system of social organization. It is important that we ask the relevant questions and not be too quick to rush in with solutions. Our minds have been trained to want answers— even before we have fully explored the questions—and that pattern keeps us immersed in the old system. To be in a state of not knowing is uncomfortable: we feel vulnerable and exposed. But, it is in this state of chaos—as in the real meaning of the word chaos, being "emptiness pregnant with possibility"— where new ideas and holistic visions can take root. Befriending chaos is one way to break old patterns and nurture the creative seed that can blossom into personal, social, and cultural transformation.

Who Is Miriam Kennet?

Miriam Kennet founded The Green Economics Institute and the *International Journal of Green Economics,* the first green academic journal. Her campaigns have been launched at the UN, in various parliaments, and at universities including Oxford, Cambridge, and Harvard. She trains, lecturers, and speaks to various governments around the globe, and also runs regular retreats on practical empowerment in economics. Miriam publishes extensively, and her work is deeply practical—reforming economics, green procurement, slow travel, green accounting, preventing poverty, harnessing and restraining corporate scope and power from within and from outside, understanding our own connection as primates and our dependence on and as part of the Earth's systems. An economist, environmental scientist, and member of the Schumacher Circle of Holistic Economists, she teaches economics at the UK's National Government School and is a member of Mansfield College and the Environmental Change Institute of Oxford University. www.greeneconomics.org.uk, greeneconomicsinstitute@yahoo.com

FIVE OF MIRIAM'S FAVORITE BOOKS:

The Third Chimpanzee, Jared Diamond

After the Ice, Steven Mithen

Feminist Economics, Edith Kuiper and Drucilla Barker

Transnational Corporations and International Production,
    Grazia Ietto-Gillies

Ecocide, Franz Broswimmer

MIRIAM
KENNET

When I was young I traveled to India and met a young boy begging on the street. His parents had removed his legs so he could beg for more money. He lived on a skateboard in a gutter by the street. My companion wanted to pay for the boy to come into a hotel to buy him dinner. But I realized—it's the system that I wanted to change—not just the moment. So I pledged to do something to change our economic system.

I campaign for social and environmental justice and to reform mainstream economics and replace it with an economics system that is accessible, diverse, and holistic.

This system I call Green Economics. It is about provisioning for the needs of all people everywhere (especially women, minorities, and people with special needs), other species, nature, the planet, and its systems.

Who Is Tama J. Kieves?

Tama J. Kieves is the bestselling author of *This Time I Dance!: Creating the Work You Love* and a sought-after speaker and career coach. She has helped thousands of individuals worldwide to discover and live their creative dreams. She is the founder of Awakening Artistry, an organization dedicated to creating a global family of visionary minds, creative souls, and empowered leaders. Her Web site offers free monthly tips for living an inspired life. www.awakeningartistry.com

FIVE BOOKS THAT HAVE INSPIRED TAMA:

A Course in Miracles, The Foundation for Inner Peace
A Return to Love, Marianne Williamson
Writing Down the Bones, Natalie Goldberg
The Artist's Way, Julia Cameron
The Essential Rumi, translated by Colman Barks

TAMA J.
KIEVES

I was a Harvard attorney at an "impressive" job, but I felt deprived and empty. When I decided to listen to the bold summons of my soul, I didn't just leave law to write. I left life as I knew it. I am committed to creating a world where everyone follows their inspired self more than their fears. It's a journey of exquisite self-trust. But should you listen to the Loving Voice within you, you will step on holy ground. There is unparalleled creativity waiting to infuse and direct you. Honor it, and it will rock your world—and ours.

Who Is Audrey E. Kitagawa?

Born and raised in Honolulu, Hawaii, Audrey is a cum laude graduate of the University of Southern California and also Boston College Law School. She practiced law in Honolulu for twenty years.

Audrey heads the Light of Awareness International Spiritual Family, a nondenominational, ecumenical, spiritual community, and she is the former adviser to the Office of the Special Representative of the Secretary General for Children and Armed Conflict at the United Nations. Currently a special adviser to the World Federation of United Nations Associations, she is now chairperson of the NGO Committee on Spirituality, Values and Global Concerns, New York, a committee of the Conference of Nongovernmental Organizations in Consultative Status with the United Nations. She is also a member of the World Wisdom Council, the World Wisdom Academy, and holds several other notable advisory positions around the world.

Audrey has been listed in *Who's Who of American Law, Who's Who of American Women, Who's Who in America, Who's Who in the World,* and *Prominent People of Hawaii.*

BOOKS THAT HAVE INSPIRED AUDREY:

Ramakrishna and His Disciples, Christopher Isherwood
The Night They Burned the Mountain, Thomas A. Dooley
Invisible Man, Ralph Ellison
Our Town, Thornton Wilder
Becket, Jean Anouilh

AUDREY E.
KITAGAWA

See the sunrise, and be filled with awe and gratitude to the Creator who paints us a new sky canvas every morning. During the day, take note of those who smile, hold open doors, and give up their seats on crowded buses. Commit to sharing with others similar acts of generosity of spirit and respect, and be that generative center of change that you want to see in the world. At sunset, be filled with wonder and peace at yet another sky canvas that whispers the coming of the evening, though filled with darkness, will be punctuated by the light of the moon and the brilliant stars that unveil a map that guides us into the unknown, waiting to be discovered.

Who Is David Korten?

David Korten is the cofounder and board chair of the Positive Futures Network, which publishes *Yes!* magazine; founder and president of the People-Centered Development Forum; a founding associate of the International Forum on Globalization; a board member of the Business Alliance for Local Living Economies; and a member of the Social Ventures Network and the Club of Rome. His books include *The Great Turning: From Empire to Earth Community, When Corporations Rule the World*, and *The Post-Corporate World: Life after Capitalism*. Korten has thirty years' experience as a development professional in Asia, Africa, and Latin America and has served as a Harvard Business School professor, a Ford Foundation project specialist, and an Asia regional adviser to USAID. www.davidkorten.org, www.greatturning.org, www.developmentforum.net, www.yesmagazine.org

FIVE BOOKS THAT HAVE SHAPED DAVID'S THINKING:
The Chalice and the Blade, Riane Eisler
The Dream of the Earth, Thomas Berry
Biology Revisioned, Willis Harman and Elisabet Sahtouris
The Rainbow and the Worm, Mae-Wan Ho
Awakening Earth, Duane Elgin

DAVID
KORTEN

We stand at a defining human moment born of a convergence of imperative and opportunity. For five thousand years, we humans have cultivated our capacities for greed and violence in a deadly competition for the power to dominate and exploit one another and Earth. Having reached the limits of exploitation that people and planet will tolerate, we face the prospect of planetary-scale social and environmental collapse. At this same precise moment, we have achieved the communications capabilities required to function as a global intelligence, cultivate our higher order capacities for love and sharing, and turn the human course as a conscious collective choice.

Who Is Stanley Krippner?

Stanley Krippner, PhD, is a professor of psychology at Saybrook University. He is the coauthor of several books, including *Personal Mythology* and *Spiritual Dimensions of Healing.* He is the recipient of the Ashley Montagu Peace Award and the American Psychological Association's Award for Contributions to the International Development of Psychology. www.stanleykrippner.weebly.com

FIVE WORKS THAT HAVE MOST INSPIRED STANLEY'S LIFE:

The Book of Job

Tao Te Ching, Lao Tzu

A Course in Miracles, The Foundation for Inner Peace

Darwin's Lost Theory of Love, David Loye

The Passionate Mind Revisited, Joel Kramer and Diana Alstad

STANLEY
KRIPPNER

My vision of hope is that the major world religions will have major reformations and revelations that will help them become part of the solution to the "world problematique" rather than part of the problem. Some of these changes have already started, with religious groups taking leadership roles in saving the environment, and in feeding, clothing, and healing needy people. A few religious groups are taking positive steps in promoting family planning, educating and empowering women, and embracing ethnic and sexual diversity. My hope is that spiritual awakening will enlighten more individuals, as well as the leaders of churches, temples, and mosques.

Who Is Satish Kumar?

Satish Kumar is an Indian, currently living in England, who has been a Jain monk and a nuclear disarmament advocate and is the current editor of *Resurgence* magazine. He is the founder and director of programs of Schumacher College, an international center for ecological studies, and the founder of the Small School. His most notable accomplishment was a "peace walk" with a companion to the capitals of four nuclear-armed countries: United States, England, France, and Russia, a trip of over eight thousand miles. He insists that reverence for nature should be at the heart of every political and social debate. www.resurgence.org

BOOKS THAT HAVE BEEN INSPIRATIONAL TO SATISH:

An Autobiography, Mahatma Gandhi
Talks on the Gita, Vinoba Bhave
Small Is Beautiful, E. F. Schumacher
Silent Spring, Rachel Carson
The Dream of the Earth, Thomas Berry

SATISH
KUMAR

The future well-being of humanity and the Earth is dependent on a new world-view in which the care of the planet, the nourishment of the soul, and the nurturing of the human community are integrated and seen as a continuum.

As the trinity of egalité, liberté, and fraternité, now we need a new trinity for the age of ecology which has wholeness, integrity, and cohesion. I propose the trinity of soil, soul, and society.

Our reverence for the Earth, our care of the soul, and a just order in society represent a vision of sustainability, spirituality, and justice.

Who Are John and Zana Lamont?

John and Zana work, both together and independently, as motivational speakers, course presenters, and facilitators, helping people achieve desired change in their lives. They work, both with groups and individuals, in a variety of health care, business, and social work settings. They are cofounders of the Western School of Professional Therapy Education. The Lamonts have written and presented courses on a wide variety of topics, including motivation for writers, presentation skills, sports therapy, and tools for life. They live together in Ayr on the west coast of Scotland, UK. www.succeedonpurpose.co.uk

FIVE BOOKS THAT HAVE INSPIRED JOHN AND ZANA:

Meditations, Marcus Aurelius
Man's Search for Meaning, Viktor Frankl
Molecules of Emotion, Candace Pert
Mapping the Mind, Rita Carter
Way of the Peaceful Warrior, Dan Millman

JOHN
AND ZANA
LAMONT

Close your eyes and picture a world where we all do our best—not just for ourselves, but for our families, our friends, our communities, and the planet.

Now picture a world where everyone knows just how powerful they *really* are—where they understand and know how to harness the unlimited potential of their minds to create their best "best" ever.

Now think of the best *you* could achieve with that power—for yourself, your family, your friends, your community, and your planet.

Who Is Peter Lang?

Peter Lang is a freelance environmental consultant and campaigner. In 1990 he cofounded Green & Away, Europe's only tented conference center that provides conference facilities close to nature for organizations and businesses. He is events director for *Resurgence* magazine and a Fellow of the Royal Society of Arts. He has written books on ethical investment and the local economy, and has worked as adviser to the Green deputy mayor of London and as press officer to the UK Green Group in the European Parliament. www.resurgence.org

BOOKS THAT HAVE INSPIRED PETER'S LIFE:
The Generous Earth, Philip Oyler
Collapse, Jared Diamond
Remarkable Trees of the World, Thomas Pakenham
How to Be Happy, Liz Hoggard

PETER
LANG

I am constantly inspired and enthused not so much by charismatic speakers on platforms or TV, but by the myriads of people who help organize environmental events and campaigns—the stewards, the ticket sellers, the caterers, the stallholders.

These are the people who work selflessly for environmental and social change. They do so willingly, mostly they do it extremely competently, and they do it with joy in their hearts. Not for the standing ovations and people queuing to talk to them afterward, but they work quietly and with determination for the Green movement—and with it they bring inspiration.

Who Is Anna Lappé?

Anna Lappé is a national bestselling author and television personality whose work focuses on food systems, sustainability, and personal health. A founding principal of the Small Planet Institute and Small Planet Fund, Anna is the coauthor of *Hope's Edge: The Next Diet for a Small Planet* and *Grub: Ideas for an Urban Organic Kitchen.* www.smallplanetinstitute.org, www.smallplanetfund.org

BOOKS THAT CHANGED ANNA'S LIFE:

Silent Spring, Rachel Carson

Trust Us, We're Experts!, John Stauber and Sheldon Rampton

Diet for a Small Planet, Frances Moore Lappé

ANNA
LAPPÉ

In an era when so much can lead us to feel hopeless, we need hope more than ever. But this unique moment calls us to a new kind of hope, not the kind we get from sticking our heads in the sand—*or* in the clouds. We need hope like that embodied in the people I've been privileged to meet around the globe, from the sweltering heat of the Punjab to the plains of Brazil to the villages south of Nairobi. In each of these places, I've met people working, against daunting odds, to transform their communities by uprooting poverty. I was shocked at first to realize these are among the most hopeful people I've ever met. Through them, I came to see that hope is not born of naiveté, or of delusion. We feel hope when we make tough choices, when we choose to become part of the struggle to make a difference no matter what the odds. This kind of hope is not what we seek in evidence; it's what we become in action. It's the hope we need for the twenty-first century.

Who Is Frances Moore Lappé?

Frances Moore Lappé is the author or coauthor of sixteen books. Her 1971 three-million-copy bestseller, *Diet for a Small Planet*, continues to awaken readers to the human-made causes of hunger and the power of our everyday choices to create the world we want. Together, Lappé and her daughter, Anna Lappé, lead the Cambridge-based Small Planet Institute, a collaborative network for research and popular education to bring democracy to life. With her daughter, she is also the cofounder of the Small Planet Fund, channeling resources to democratic social movements worldwide. Her most recent book is *Getting a Grip: Clarity, Creativity & Courage in a World Gone Mad*. Lappé is the winner of the Right Livelihood Award, sometimes called the Alternative Nobel, and is a founding councilor of the World Future Council. www.smallplanetinstitute.org

INFLUENTIAL BOOKS FOR FRANCES:

The Anatomy of Human Destructiveness, Erich Fromm

The Great Transformation, Karl Polanyi

An Interrupted Life, Etty Hillesum

Thoughts without a Thinker, Mark Epstein

The Hungry Planet, Georg Borgstrom

FRANCES
MOORE
LAPPÉ

People often ask, "What do I matter? I'm just a drop in the bucket." But the problem isn't being a drop—for buckets fill up pretty fast on rainy nights. So, to find our power, we must ask, "Why are things the way they are?" Then, we can target our actions so we see them filling up the bucket. A root cause of suffering in our world today is the underlying premise of lack—the lack of goods and goodness: there is just not enough to go around, we're told, and we humans are merely selfish and materialistic. If we believe this, we are powerless! But, we embody the deep human needs for connection, fairness, and meaning. And when we put a lie to the premise of lack, we discover our power, and simultaneously we uproot the causes of needless suffering. What glorious "drops" we then become!

Who Is Jeremy Leggett?

Social entrepreneur Jeremy Leggett is the founder and executive chairman of Solarcentury, a leading European solar energy company; and the founder and chairman of SolarAid, a charity set up with 5 percent of Solarcentury profits. He is also a founding director of the world's first private equity investment fund for renewables, run by Bank Sarasin. He has written several books, including *The Carbon War, Half Gone,* and *The Solar Century.* www.jeremy.leggett.net

FIVE BOOKS THAT IMPACTED JEREMY'S LIFE:

The Tipping Point, Malcolm Gladwell
Financing Change, Stephan Schmidheiny
The Innovator's Dilemma, Clayton Christensen
Earth in the Balance, Al Gore
Fool's Gold, Gillian Tett

JEREMY
LEGGETT

I've been thinking about a way to save the world while opting out of the broken system that is destroying it. Rates-of-return on investments in renewables projects are now higher than any bank will offer on a savings account. Yet many developers of renewables projects cannot get credit from the banks to build their projects. In the bankers' dysfunctional world, the risk is too high. It isn't. So, I say, let's drop the bonus cultists who are wrecking the planet. Let's we the people do the bankrolling and developing of clean-energy projects. Let's create a people-power phenomenon using the Internet.

Who Is Scott London?

Scott London is a California-based journalist and radio presenter. He is perhaps best known as the host of *Insight & Outlook,* a cultural affairs program heard on National Public Radio stations in the United States and on global shortwave. Over the past two decades, he has charted emerging trends and profiled outstanding and innovative thinkers in many fields. His interviews and commentaries have been widely broadcast and have appeared in books, journals, and magazines worldwide. Raised and educated in Sweden, he has lived in the United States since 1990. www.scottlondon.com

GREAT BOOKS THAT HAVE UPLIFTED SCOTT'S LIFE:

The Perennial Philosophy, Aldous Huxley

Autobiography of a Yogi, Paramahansa Yogananda

The Transformations of Man, Lewis Mumford

The Passion of the Western Mind, Richard Tarnas

An Intimate History of Humanity, Theodore Zeldin

SCOTT
LONDON

People often define genius as a set of character traits or a way of being. Books instruct us on how to think like Einstein or Leonardo da Vinci. But I see genius as the fulfillment of our true calling in life, as the flowering of our unique potential, whatever it happens to be. What good is thinking like an Einstein if you're a Picasso or a Charlie Chaplin? Why act like a Mozart if you're a Maya Lin or a Tiger Woods? Every genius inhabits a universe of his or her own making, so imitating the behavior of others is pointless.

Who Is Diana Loomans?

Diana Loomans is a national speaker, bestselling author, journalist, and founder of the Quantum Life Institute in Los Angeles. For over twenty years, Diana has been inspiring entrepreneurs, leaders, educators, and parents to tap into more of their greatness and to make a positive difference in the world. A former university instructor, Diana leads workshops and retreats on topics including maximizing potential, innovative thinking, and creating an awakened world. She champions causes ranging from raising conscious children to raising environmental awareness. Diana is the founder of People Making a Difference, a campaign that inspires people to give back 1 percent of their time in service to the world. www.dianaloomans.com, www.quantumlifeinstitute.com

BOOKS THAT HAVE INSPIRED DIANA'S LIFE:
The Highly Sensitive Person, Elaine Aron
Make Your Creative Dreams Real, SARK
One Day My Soul Just Opened Up, Iyanla Vanzant
The Freedom Writers Diary, The Freedom Writers and Erin Gruwell
In the Spirit, Susan Taylor

DIANA
LOOMANS

AN AWAKENED WORLD

Imagine an Awakened World, where every precious child is born welcomed and loved. A world where all colors and creeds are celebrated as one brilliant bouquet of flowering Humanity. A world where people are making a difference for a living, and living to make a difference.

Imagine an Awakened World that has shifted from the overpowering of some, to the empowering of all. A world where human force is met with soul force; one that knows there are no sides to a planet that is round. A world where true religion is recognized simply as kindness, and one great circle of Love honoring the Creator.

Imagine an Awakened World, where everyone knows that world peace begins with inner peace, and that one conscious person can awaken millions.

Who Is David Lorimer?

David Lorimer is a writer, lecturer, and editor who is also the program director of the Scientific and Medical Network and was formerly a teacher of languages and philosophy at Winchester College. He is the author and editor
of twelve books, including *Radical Prince, Thinking beyond the Brain*, and
Science, Consciousness and Ultimate Reality. He is the vice president of the
Swedenborg Society and of Wrekin Trust, a charity dedicated to supporting
deeper spiritual connection. He is also a member of the International Futures Forum and the editor of its digest, *Omnipedia—Thinking for Tomorrow.*
www.learningforlife.org.uk, www.davidlorimer.net, www.scimednet.org, www
.internationalfuturesforum.com, www.ufsforum.org

INFLUENTIAL BOOKS:

The Wellspring of Good, Peter Deunov
My Childhood and Youth, Albert Schweitzer
Knowledge and the Sacred, Seyyed Hossein Nasr
The Passion of the Western Mind, Richard Tarnas
The Ways and Power of Love, Pitirim Sorokin

DAVID
LORIMER

"Be wise as serpents and gentle as doves."—Jesus of Nazareth

The world is moving, slowly but inexorably, toward a Culture of Love, the human expression of the Oneness of Life. Many individuals have realized the futility of the vicious cycle of violence as expressed in the "war on terror" that fuels a world system based on fear and manipulative control and supports the continued research and production of arms in the name of security. Security is based on fear while peace is based on love. Visionaries are realists, but are not consumed by rage. Their energy, rather, is oriented toward cocreating a new world based on love, wisdom, truth, peace, and justice.

Who Is Caroline Lucas?

Caroline has been a Green Party member of the European Parliament for southeast England since 1999, having previously served as the Green Party's first county councilor on Oxfordshire County Council, UK. She is a member of the European Parliament's Environmental, International Trade, and Climate Change committees. She is a cofounder and co-president of the cross-party group on peace initiatives and vice president of the cross-party groups on consumer affairs and animal rights. In 2006 she was short-listed for the *New Statesman*'s Person of the Year poll; in 2007 she was short-listed for the *Observer* newspaper's Ethical Politician of the Year award. Caroline is vice president of the Royal Society for the Prevention of Cruelty to Animals (RSPCA) and the Stop the War Coalition. She is also a member of the decision-making National Council of the Campaign for Nuclear Disarmament. www.carolinelucasmep.org.uk

FIVE OF CAROLINE'S FAVORITE BOOKS:

Small Is Beautiful, E. F. Schumacher

Seeing Green, Jonathon Porritt

Fighting for Hope, Petra Kelly

Gift from the Sea, Anne Morrow Lindbergh

Journal of a Solitude, May Sarton

CAROLINE
LUCAS

I dream of a time when humanity lives in harmony with the world around us, and with each other. Such harmony would make the acquisition of weapons of mass destruction unthinkable, and lead to an economic system that, instead of destroying the planet, is genuinely based on social and environmental justice. But it's more than a dream. People are increasingly turning to Green politics, the politics of life, and striving to turn this dream into reality. For me, that's the greatest inspiration: that future generations will still have a chance to live in harmony with the world. So dream and act!

Who Is Gay Luce?

Gay Luce, PhD, a Radcliffe and Stanford graduate and once a writer for President Kennedy's Scientific Advisory Committee, has become a choreographer of spiritual transformation, thanks to great teachers such as Rinpoche Tarthang Tulku and Richard Moss. Gay drew attention to the needs of aging people by starting Senior Actualization and Growth Exploration (SAGE). In 1985 she began the Nine Gates Mystery School, an intense experiential program with teachers from many of the world's great spiritual traditions. Five years ago a Nine Gates program for teens demonstrated how touchingly responsive youth are to spiritual experience. Now a children's program is in the works. www.ninegates.org

THE FOLLOWING BOOKS HAVE BEEN A MAJOR INFLUENCE ON GAY'S JOURNEY:

Gesture of Balance, Tarthang Tulku
Pointing Out the Great Way, Daniel P. Brown
Three Cups of Tea, Greg Mortenson and David Oliver Relin
The Tibetan Book of Living and Dying, Soygal Rinpoche
Fire in the Heart, Kyriacos Markides

GAY
LUCE

For an optimistic future, let us strive to be good people.

Attunement to each other, nature, and Spirit seem to me an essential anti-dote to the unconsciousness and dissociation that have brought us humans to our current precipice.

Our problems will be solved according to how well we each hone our own character to be honest, compassionate, inclusive, etc., whatever our age. But to benefit the future we need to listen deeply to our children. Love them without conditions. Give them tools for deep inner sight, awareness of self and other, and educate them in the inherently tantric dance of life, so they know that even the slightest thought has consequences, and the inner worlds are far bigger than the outer.

Who Is Mark Lynas?

Mark Lynas is the author of three books on climate change: *High Tide: News from a Warming World, The Carbon Calculator,* and *Six Degrees: Our Future on a Hotter Planet,* which won the Royal Society Prize for Science Books. Both *High Tide* and *Six Degrees* have been translated into more than fifteen languages. *Six Degrees* was also made into a television documentary, broadcast around the world to an audience of many millions via the National Geographic Channel. Mark is a well-known international public speaker and a frequent contributor to *The Guardian* and *The Independent* newspapers. www.marklynas.org

FIVE BOOKS THAT HAVE INSPIRED MARK:

Dinosaurs and All that Rubbish, Michael Foreman
The Ages of Gaia, James Lovelock
Things Fall Apart, Chinua Achebe
Last Chance to See, Douglas Adams
A Confederacy of Dunces, John Kennedy Toole

MARK
LYNAS

Humans have become a geologically potent force on our planet. We are now changing the chemistry and biology of our oceans and atmosphere more dramatically than the fiercest hurricane or most powerful volcano. Our reign might be short—an anomalous interval characterized by the Earth's sixth major mass extinction, and ending in our own demise. Or we might reconcile ourselves to the realities of living on a limited, crowded planet and learn to flourish within the everlasting capacity of the biosphere to renew itself. Either option is open to us—but we don't have long to decide which outcome we want.

Who Is Tim Mack?

Tim Mack has edited *Futures Research Quarterly* for twenty-two years and is now president of the World Future Society. After holding research positions at the Kennedy School of Government at Harvard and the National Academy of Sciences, Tim Mack joined the U.S. General Accounting Office as part of the Budget Policy Task Force. He also served on the Board of the MIT Enterprise Forum and as a vice president at WPP Ltd., one of the largest management consulting and market communications companies in the world. He is a member of the New York and District of Columbia bars.

BOOKS THAT HAVE INSPIRED TIM:

The Wind-Up Bird Chronicle, Haruki Murakami
The Evolution of Future Consciousness, Thomas Lombardo
The Study of the Future, Edward Cornish
Zen and the Art of Motorcycle Maintenance, Robert Pirsig
The Power of One, Bryce Courtenay

TIM
MACK

Our modern world is no longer an unconnected collection of parts but an integrated whole, where myriads of factors shape the unfolding future. With dizzying and accelerating speed, each innovation provides a new platform for dozens more; but the unintended consequences of new technologies, misunderstandings among cultures and religions, and the failures of spiritual and creative imagination are always looming on the horizon. In spite of this, humanity has a history of hair's breadth escapes from disaster, the heroic overcoming of insurmountables, and rebirth after catastrophe. Goodwill, thoughtful care, and enduring effort remain the positive wellsprings of the future.

Who Is Peter Madden?

Peter Madden is the chief executive of Forum for the Future. Previously, he worked as head of policy at the Environment Agency. Prior to that, he was ministerial adviser at the Department for Environment, Food and Rural Affairs (Defra), director of Green Alliance, and head of policy at Christian Aid. He is also a board member of Groundwork UK. www.forumforthefuture.org.uk

PETER'S FAVORITE BOOKS:

Brave New World, Aldous Huxley

Neuromancer, William Gibson

For the Common Good, Herman Daly and John Cobb, Jr.

The Politics of the Real World, Michael Jacobs

Natural Capitalism, Paul Hawken, Amory B. Lovins, and L. Hunter Lovins

PETER
MADDEN

The future is a place of opportunity, where things can grow and prosper, where knowledge will spread, and creativity and innovation should flourish. Yet too many green visions are apocalyptic, doom-laden, and deterministic. Enough gloominess! We need to inspire and challenge people with positive stories of a sustainable future. Being green is not a brake on progress but synonymous with good economic sense and all the ingredients of a happy life. A sustainable future can be achieved. It is the only way business and communities will prosper. We need bold action now to make it happen.

Who Is Shakti Maira?

Shakti Maira is a painter, sculptor, and author based in New Delhi, India. His art is connected with spirituality, and he has had exhibitions in India, the United States, and Europe, of which twenty-five have been one-person shows. He has written *Towards Ananda: Rethinking Indian Art and Aesthetics,* and his articles and columns have appeared in *The Hindu, The Times of India, First City* and *Design Today.* He has been engaged with art education for children and was invited by UNESCO to write the Asian vision statement for Arts in Education: Learning through the Arts. www.shaktimaira.com

FIVE BOOKS THAT ENRICHED SHAKTI'S LIFE:
The Prophet, Kahlil Gibran
An Experiment in Mindfulness, E. H. Shattock
The Experience of Insight, Joseph Goldstein
An Autobiography, Mahatma Gandhi
No Boundary, Ken Wilber

SHAKTI
MAIRA

Let's go beyond this current confusion about beauty and aesthetics, as they are vital paths to well-being and happiness.

Beauty is not superficial prettiness, nor the property of objects. Beauty is an experience and is at its heart about relationship. When relationships, outer and inner, have harmony, balance, rhythm, and proportionality, there is beauty and joy—whether in the form of a pot or a building with its immediate ecology, or in social systems that deliver justice and peace.

We must all be artists—sensitive to the web of inter-relationships that is life and passionately attentive to beauty and its creation.

Who Is Raymond A. Mar?

Raymond A. Mar is an assistant professor at York University in the Department of Psychology in Toronto, Canada. His work has appeared in various journals including *Neuropsychologia, Journal of Research in Personality, Social Cognitive and Affective Neuroscience, Perspectives on Psychological Science,* and in the book *Empathy and Fairness.* The central topic of his research is the simulation of social experience afforded by fictional narratives such as literature, cinema, and theater. www.utoronto.ca

PEOPLE WHOSE WORKS DEEPLY INSPIRED RAYMOND:

From the world of cinema: Kiyoshi Kurosawa, Tsai Ming-liang, Park Chanwook, Wong Kar-wai, Lars von Trier, and Peter Greenaway. From music: Stevie Wonder, Marvin Gaye, John Coltrane, Nina Simone, Leroy Hutson, Charles Mingus, Max Roach, Al Green, Chick Corea, and Cannonball Adderley. And from literature: W. G. Sebald, Chris Ware, Franz Kafka, Yukio Mishima, Sheila Heti, and Anthony Bourdain.

RAYMOND A.
MAR

If you allow yourself the luxury of observation, you will find the world around you to be a marvelous place. Our physical world boasts great beauty without intention, often discarded at the intersection of man and nature. And our social world plays out in a far more strange and amusing manner than we could ever fabricate. So pay attention. I don't think we'll be coming back this way again.

Who Is Robert W. McChesney?

Robert W. McChesney is the Gutgsell Endowed Professor in the Department of Communication at the University of Illinois at Urbana-Champaign. In 2008 *Utne Reader* listed McChesney among its fifty visionaries who are changing the world. He is the cofounder of Free Press, the U.S. media reform organization with over five hundred thousand members. McChesney has written or edited seventeen books, and his work has been translated into eighteen languages. His most recent book is *The Death and Life of American Journalism: The Media Revolution that Will Begin the World Again*. www.robertmcchesney.com

FIVE BOOKS THAT HAVE INSPIRED ROBERT:

Monopoly Capital, Paul Baran and Paul Sweezy

Advertising on Trial, Inger Stole

Marx's Ecology, John Bellamy Foster

Manufacturing Consent, Edward Herman and Noam Chomsky

The Genius of Impeachment, John Nichols

ROBERT W.
MCCHESNEY

The profit system is no longer a viable option for humanity, as our environment crumbles, inequality deepens, militarism expands, and, caught in a rat race, humanity is detached and dispirited. We are at a juncture where we can take the truly revolutionary step of advancing to a higher stage of human development or we can participate in a descent into high-tech barbarism. In the midst of our technological revolution, we have the capacity to have media that deepen democracy or that contribute to mindless plutocracy. I am optimistic about our future, because only a few benefit from the status quo—and even then, only in a narrow sense. We have the power to determine our fate.

Who Are Corinne McLaughlin and Gordon Davidson?

Corinne McLaughlin and Gordon Davidson are the coauthors of *Spiritual Politics: Changing the World from the Inside Out* and cofounders of the Center for Visionary Leadership. Corinne coordinated a national task force for President Clinton's Council on Sustainable Development, and Gordon was executive director of the Social Investment Forum. www.visionarylead.org

CORINNE
MCLAUGHLIN
AND GORDON
DAVIDSON

SPIRITUAL POLITICS FOR THE TWENTY-FIRST CENTURY

True spirituality can ennoble politics, and politics can ground spirituality. Some key approaches in spiritual politics emerging today are:

1. Searching for common ground to resolve conflicts: using professionally facilitated, multi-stakeholder dialogues to make public policy help us understand the differences, while acting on the commonalities.

2. Transforming negative thinking, as consciousness is causal: exploring how our collective thoughts are affecting our collective social health.

3. Using meditation and prayer to invoke the soul of a nation and spiritual support: asking for help from higher dimensions, as we humans do not have to struggle with our problems alone—help is always available.

Who Is Lynne McTaggart?

Lynne McTaggart is an internationally recognized spokesperson on the science of spirituality and is the award-winning author of five books, including *The Field* and *The Intention Experiment*, which have now been globally published in over seventeen languages. Through her Web site, Lynne periodically invites her readers to take part in the world's largest studies of mass intention with noted scientists in consciousness research. She is the editor of *Living the Field,* an audio course that helps to bring the science of *The Field* into everyday life. She also holds Living the Field seminars around the world. www.livingthefield.com, www.theintentionexperiment.com

FIVE BOOKS THAT HAVE DEFINED LYNNE:

Slouching Towards Bethlehem, Joan Didion
In Cold Blood, Truman Capote
Confessions of a Medical Heretic, Robert Mendelsohn, MD
All the President's Men, Bob Woodward and Carl Bernstein
To the Lighthouse, Virginia Woolf

LYNNE
MCTAGGART

Although we perceive science as an ultimate truth, science is finally just a story, told in installments. The latest chapter, written by a group of frontier scientific explorers, suggests that at our essence we exist as a unity, a relationship utterly interdependent, the parts affecting the whole at every moment.

The implications of this new story on the design of our society are extraordinary. If we're not separate, we need to redefine what we designate as me and not-me. We have to reconsider how we choose and carry out our work, structure our communities, and bring up our children. We have to imagine another way to live, an entirely new way to be.

Who Is Bazil Meade?

Bazil has been the driving force behind the upsurge in UK gospel music for the past thirty years. He initiated the most famous gospel choir in Europe, the London Community Gospel Choir (LCGC), which he leads. The choir's popularity has enabled them to visit many countries in Europe, Asia, Africa, and the Caribbean. LCGC has collaborated with many famous artists from around the world, such as Beverley Knight, Elton John, Stevie Wonder, and Luther Vandross. Bazil is known for nurturing singers and musicians through LCGC. Many pop and R&B bands, churches, and West End productions have been inspired by Bazil's style of gospel music. He continues to lead UK gospel from the front. Bazil believes in the power of gospel music to bring about change and has a vision to establish an academy to be a hub for gospel music in Europe. He has pioneered gospel choirs in many schools around the world, and he is in great demand for gospel vocal coaching with his master classes, which are run across Europe. www.lcgc.org.uk

BAZIL'S FAVORITE BOOKS:

The Bible

Feel the Fear and Do It Anyway, Susan Jeffers

BAZIL'S FAVORITE SONGS:

"Everything Must Change," sung by George Benson

"Maggie May," Rod Stewart

"A Song for You," Donny Hathaway

BAZIL
MEADE

THE HUMAN SPIRIT THROUGH THE EYES OF A MUSICIAN

The coming together of people to celebrate a common interest such as music brings a oneness and unity of spirit seldom seen but comparable to the camaraderie felt at large sporting events. To be instrumental in bringing about this harmony between people, be it from different countries, faiths, or social standing, gives purpose and reason to life.

The "adrenaline junkie," such as a parachutist, gets no bigger rush than the musician who lives for those special moments when an audience is totally absorbed, enthralled in rhythm, singing and clapping. For that reason, music is played or sung to unite the heart, emotion, and spirit of the audience into one powerful expression of human joy and appreciation for that priceless God-given gift—music.

Who Is Dan Millman?

Dan Millman, a former world-champion athlete, university coach, martial arts instructor, and college professor, is the author of thirteen books, including *Way of the Peaceful Warrior, Wisdom of the Peaceful Warrior, Sacred Journey of the Peaceful Warrior, The Life You Were Born to Live, No Ordinary Moments, The Laws of Spirit,* and T*he Journeys of Socrates.* His books have inspired millions of readers in twenty-nine languages. The feature film *Peaceful Warrior* is based on Dan's early life. His talks and trainings have influenced leaders in the fields of health, psychology, education, business, sports, and the arts. Married for over thirty years, Dan is the proud father of three daughters and grandfather of two grandsons. www.danmillman.com, www.peacefulwarrior.com

BOOKS THAT HAVE INFLUENCED AND INSPIRED DAN'S LIFE:

Constructive Living, David K. Reynolds

Siddhartha, Hermann Hesse

The Lord of the Rings, J. R. R. Tolkien

DAN
MILLMAN

Do we have to quiet our minds, think positive thoughts, and feel the right emotions in order to live well? I suggest another way—the peaceful warrior's way of action. We can cease our struggle to fix our insides, accept our thoughts and feelings (positive or negative), while doing constructive, purposeful action. We can behave with courage and kindness, whether or not we feel that way. We can turn what we know into what we do. Here. Now. We are, each and all, peaceful warriors in training, learning to live with a peaceful heart and a warrior spirit.

Who Is Charles Montagu?

Charles Montagu was the first hypnotherapist funded by the National Health Service (NHS). He sits on the boards of the British Institute for Complementary Medicine and the American Council of Hypnotist Examiners. He is a trustee of Crossroads Centre in Antigua and numerous other charities. He conducts workshops internationally and is the cofounder of the Health Partnership, an integrative medical and holistic center in central London, where he practices.

INSPIRATION FOR CHARLES:
The Prophet, Kahlil Gibran
Infinite Happiness, Masami Saionji
Emotional Resilience, David Viscott, MD

CHARLES
MONTAGU

We are one. We may *think* differently, yet each of us is, in essence, the same. So let us lose our minds … and come to our senses! All conflict can be healed with love, acceptance, and by striving to understand the perception of another.

Remember, our love ability is boundless. At heart we are all of us, as children, expert at being fully alive. We heal as we remember *who we are.*

As we heal the division between our hearts and our minds, we can truly unite for the good of all humankind.

Who Is Lady Fiona Montagu?

Lady Fiona Montagu of Beaulieu, born in Zimbabwe, is a director of Beaulieu Enterprises Ltd. She was appointed as first global ambassador to the Club of Budapest. She is an international adviser to Nobel Peace Laureate Betty Williams's World Centres of Compassion for Children. She is also on the advisory board for KidsRights and a member of the World Wisdom Council, created, amongst other aims, to improve global ethics especially in the media.

Fiona Montagu is dedicated to the human future, is patron of many charities, such as the Hunger Project, and studies practical metaphysics with a view to raising global consciousness by building bridges of awareness, compassion, and cooperation between the nations of our planet. Her metaphysical coworker is Gillian R. Wright. www.beaulieu.co.uk, www.lucid-living.com, www.wccci.org, www.kidsrights.info

BOOKS THAT HAVE MOST INFLUENCED LADY FIONA'S EVOLUTIONARY JOURNEY:

The Interconnected Universe, Ervin Laszlo
Remembrance of Things Past, Marcel Proust
Many works by Alice Bailey

LADY FIONA
MONTAGU

A new quality of planetary imagination is demanded from all of us as the price of human survival. Focused, determined, enlightened public opinion is the most potent force in the world. The real catastrophe out there is poverty—spiritual poverty and the poverty of the imagination.

Who Is Thomas Moore?

Thomas Moore has been a monk, a musician, a professor of religion, a psychotherapist, and a full-time writer and lecturer. His most well-known book is *Care of the Soul.* Today he fits no categories of belief or affiliation, religious or professional, but his work breathes with the spirit of Ralph Waldo Emerson, William Blake, and William Morris. www.careofthesoul.net

FIVE BOOKS THAT HAVE MOST SHAPED THOMAS'S VISION:

Zen Mind, Beginner's Mind, Shunryu Suzuki

Re-Visioning Psychology, James Hillman

The Book of Life, Marsilio Ficino

Memories, Dreams, Reflections, C. G. Jung

Letters of Emily Dickinson

THOMAS
MOORE

We are slowly heading toward a future when war will seem unthinkable, illness will be understood as an affliction of the soul and spirit as well as the body, and education will be based in joy rather than punishment.

Our most important challenge now is to embrace our full sexuality and dedicate ourselves to art, dream, beauty, and sensual delight. As people, we are not made up of brain cells and genes; we are bodies ensouled, created for the entertainment of ideas and sensations.

Who Is Tyler Moorehead?

Tyler Moorehead is the chief executive of Big Picture Group (www.bigpicture. tv). She has over twenty years' experience in media and campaigns, including five years as the publisher of the world's largest environmental magazine, *The Ecologist*. Tyler is a columnist for several magazines, and has advised the World Bank, UK Department of the Environment, PLAN International, and companies in retail, construction, fashion, and packaging. She has led international advocacy for the UN/World Bank–sponsored International Assessment of Agricultural Science & Technology for Development (IAASTD), and the international congress for a Blueprint on Agriculture for the Soil Association. Tyler sits on the COM Plus steering committee led by the UN Environment Programme (UNEP), and was recently appointed UK representative for Cradle 2 Cradle design. www.bigpicture.tv

FIVE BOOKS THAT INSPIRED TYLER:

Small Is Beautiful, E. F. Schumacher
The Man Who Planted Trees, Jean Giono
Democracy in America, Alexis de Tocqueville
Silent Spring, Rachel Carson
The Lorax, Dr. Seuss

TYLER
MOOREHEAD

We proclaim, "Let the people speak!" and search for an "authentic" voice to represent thousands more. Perhaps we've missed the point. To speak out is to share ourselves as individuals—a profound act of citizenship and community. When we speak, we take ownership of our values and declare boundaries; we connect our words to our deeds. We speak to be acknowledged, and so find our humanity. An engaged and humane society is our best hope for the future. E.F. Schumacher said, "People willing to speak up are people willing to act up." Self-expression is leadership. If we want leaders, then we must "let the people speak!"

Who Is Bill Mosher?

Bill Mosher is an award-winning writer, seasoned documentary filmmaker, accomplished landscape painter, and an emerging sculptor. At twenty-eight years old, without any formal training as a writer, he founded a small-town weekly newspaper where he won prestigious awards in investigative reporting and feature writing. In 1992 he started his first television series, *Worldscape,* hosted by Walter Cronkite. The series was designed to inspire young artists to paint directly from nature, and during its production, Mosher learned to paint. In 1993 Mosher founded Visionaries, a nonprofit organization dedicated to using the power of media to inspire positive social change. The main focus has been the production of the *Visionaries* television series, and over the last dozen years, it has become one of the most acclaimed nonprofit media projects in the world, having produced more than 140 documentaries in fifty countries. Bill Mosher lives on Cape Cod with his wife, Christine; his daughter, Michelle; and son Mike. His oldest son, Matthew, is an aspiring screenwriter and college professor in Boston, Massachusetts. www.visionaries.org

FIVE FAVORITE BOOKS THAT HAVE INSPIRED BILL:

The City of Joy, Dominique Lapierre
Guns, Germs, and Steel, Jared Diamond
Drawing on the Right Side of the Brain, Betty Edwards
Consilience, Edward O. Wilson
The Art Spirit, Robert Henri

BILL
MOSHER

What do Jesus, Galileo, Gandhi, Winston Churchill, and Martin Luther King, Jr. have in common? They were storytellers. It begins with a dawning moment. There is only one God; the Earth is round; all men are created equal. Once conceived, the story takes up residence inside your brain. There it exists as a living entity. It will grow and prosper or wither and die based on two factors. The first is the magnitude of the paradigm shift. Epiphanies are not easily forgotten. The second is the power it has to evoke positive emotion. If you want to change the world, become a storyteller.

Who Is Caroline Myss?

Caroline M. Myss is the founder of CMED: Caroline Myss Education. She is the author of several life-changing books, including *Entering the Castle, Anatomy of the Spirit, Sacred Contracts, Why People Don't Heal, Invisible Acts of Power*, and the coauthor, along with C. Norman Shealy, MD, PhD, of *The Creation of Health*. www.myss.com

FIVE OF CAROLINE'S FAVORITE BOOKS:

Alice's Adventures in Wonderland and
   Through the Looking-Glass and What Alice Found There, Lewis Carroll
Team of Rivals, Doris Kearns Goodwin
The Pillars of the Earth, Ken Follett
The Interior Castle, St. Teresa of Avila
The Mists of Avalon, Marion Zimmer Bradley

CAROLINE
MYSS

We are living at an unrivaled time of change. We now live in the age of energy, of timeless global communication. Change is not only instantaneous, but it reaches all of us immediately. And change is penetrating now, melting into our psyches, our intellects, our hearts, and our souls. This is the alchemy that defines our time; this is the alchemy of a mystical renaissance, an alchemy that can initiate as much external chaos as internal awakening. When I think about a vision for the future, I see the chaos very clearly on the planet—and I see the possibility of great soul awakenings.

Who Is David Nicholson-Lord?

David Nicholson-Lord is an environmental writer, formerly with the UK-based newspapers *The Times, The Independent,* and *The Independent on Sunday,* where he was environmental editor. He has contributed to the globally renowned *Resurgence* magazine for many years and is the author of several books, including *The Greening of the Cities* and *Green Cities: And Why We Need Them.* He is the chair of the Urban Wildlife Network, deputy chair of the New Economics Foundation, and research associate for the Optimum Population Trust. He also teaches environmental studies at the City University, London, and is a member of the UNESCO UK Man and the Biosphere Forum. www.optimumpopulation.org, www.ukmaburbanforum.org.uk

FIVE BOOKS THAT HAVE INSPIRED DAVID:

Ancient Futures, Helena Norberg-Hodge
The Varieties of Religious Experience, William James
A Green History of the World, Clive Ponting
Poems, Gerard Manley Hopkins
Collapse, Jared Diamond

DAVID
NICHOLSON-
LORD

Reconnect.

Restore rivers. Regrow forests. Rebuild soils. Remake cities. Recreate wild.
Renew land, earth, air, seas, oceans.
Reduce our numbers, impact, appetites. Restrain our egos.
   Regain our humility.
Rethink our wants and needs. Reject cruelty, arrogance,
   aggression, dominance.
Rejoin the community of living creatures. Replant hope, trust, altruism.
Relearn the language of other life forms. Recover their knowledge, vision.
Reinhabit their lives. Reimagine ourselves into the fabric of the universe.
Rediscover otherness, awe, mystery, beauty, wonder.

Who Is Helena Norberg-Hodge?

Helena Norberg-Hodge is an internationally recognized pioneer of the world-wide localization movement and a leading analyst of the impact of the global economy on culture and agriculture. Fluent in seven languages, she is the author of numerous works, including *Bringing the Food Economy Home* and *Ancient Futures: Learning from Ladakh*, which, together with a film of the same name, has been translated into more than fifty languages. She is a recipient of the Alternative Nobel Prize, a founder of the International Forum on Globalization, and director of the International Society for Ecology and Culture (ISEC), renowned for its groundbreaking work on localization in Ladakh, or little Tibet. www.isec.org.uk

FIVE BOOKS THAT HAVE INSPIRED HELENA:

Small Is Beautiful, E. F. Schumacher
The Tao of Physics, Fritjof Capra
To Have or to Be?, Erich Fromm
Psychotherapy East and West, Alan Watts
The Unsettling of America, Wendell Berry

HELENA
NORBERG-
HODGE

The crises around us are mounting. The good news is that we can do something about them. The key is to realize that they are *linked*—linked to the policies of economic globalization that push business to become ever larger, in the process destroying diversity, democracy, and community. Once we recognize this underlying root cause, we can move beyond treating symptoms to tackle a range of problems at once, from pollution and climate chaos to poverty. As a matter of priority, we can join others in creating a global movement for *localization*, and thereby rebuild the fabric of ecosystems and communities.

Who Is Christiane Northrup?

Christiane Northrup, MD, is a board-certified obstetrician gynecologist, author, and beloved authority on women's health and wellness. Her three books *Women's Bodies, Women's Wisdom; The Wisdom of Menopause;* and *Mother-Daughter Wisdom* are considered classics in the field of mind/body medicine for women and have been translated into over seventeen languages. Dr. Northrup says, "The processes of the female body contain a vast amount of wisdom that we can use to guide our lives. I've spent the first half of my life studying everything that can wrong with the female body. The second half is dedicated to illuminating and affirming everything that can go right with this body." Hence the title of her fourth book, *The Secret Pleasures of Menopause.* www.drnorthrup.com

FIVE OF CHRISTIANE'S FAVORITE BOOKS:
Rediscovering the Angels and Natives of Eternity, Flower Newhouse
The Dynamic Laws of Healing, Catherine Ponder
You Can Heal Your Life, Louise Hay
Love Without End, Glenda Green
The Treasure of El Dorado, Joseph Whitfield

CHRISTIANE
NORTHRUP

When I was a medical student, I saw my first birth. And burst into tears. Nothing had prepared me for the holiness of that moment. The room was full of angels. Childbirth is the physical metaphor for how spirit comes into matter—a process that is meant to be orgasmically blissful. We are collectively being called upon to work through our birth trauma, a process that works best in an atmosphere of joy, pleasure, and love. The "no pain, no gain" approach to birth and life is now outmoded. Joy and ecstasy are the path to healing.

Who Is James O'Dea?

James O'Dea is a former president of the Institute of Noetic Sciences, which seeks to advance the science of consciousness and human experience to serve individual and collective transformation. He directed Amnesty International's Washington office for ten years and was the executive director of the Seva Foundation. He also founded and co-led international Compassion and Social Healing dialogues. James speaks across the globe on themes related to science and the evolution of consciousness and the quest for individual and global healing. www.noetic.org

BOOKS THAT HAVE INSPIRED JAMES:

Narziss and Goldmund, Hermann Hesse
A Portrait of the Artist as a Young Man, James Joyce
Complete Works, T. S. Eliot
The Collected Works, William Butler Yeats
The Possible Human, Jean Houston

JAMES
O'DEA

It is said that in those mythic beginnings when Adam and Eve were expelled from the Garden of Eden, a flaming sword was placed at the entrance to the East Gate to guard the way to the Tree of Life.

This sword is the searing mirror of perfect justice. It will burn with nonjudgment, with fearless generosity, with all-encompassing compassion. The fire of Love will burn away every contortion of your mind, every shred of guilt, blame, and inadequacy. The fire is unbearable to those who, in their own consciousness, are not ready for its absolute forgiveness, its acceptance, and its annihilation of vengeance and punishment.

At last science and spirituality can together cry out: Enter by the East Gate!

Who Is Ben Okri?

Ben Okri has published eight novels, including *The Famished Road,* as well as collections of poetry, short stories, and essays. His work has been translated into more than twenty languages. He is a Fellow of the Royal Society of Literature and has been awarded the OBE as well as numerous international prizes, including the Commonwealth Writers Prize for Africa, the Aga Khan Prize for Fiction, and the Chianti Ruffino Antico Fattore. He is a vice president of the English Centre of International PEN and was presented with a Crystal Award by the World Economic Forum. He was born in Nigeria and lives in London.

FIVE BOOKS THAT HAVE DEEPLY IMPACTED BEN'S LIFE JOURNEY:

Tao Te Ching, Lao Tzu

The Bible

The Odyssey, Homer

Don Quixote, Miguel de Cervantes

Arabian Nights, Andrew Lang

BEN
OKRI

The time will come when we will remember what our life is for. We will become poems. We will return the sacred to the ordinary, and yield the ordinary to the sacred. We will know that war with others is war with ourselves. We will see that all things, and all peoples, are connected. We will learn that love is the greatest power, and hate the greatest weakness. We will respect the Earth as we respect our body. We will use imagination to banish hunger. Our science will be prophetic, and our prophecy scientific. We will breathe better.

We will see that everything is touched with an essential magic. Our awakening will liberate the future. We will become higher dreamers again, and coworkers in the creation of a new universal civilization.

Who Is Judith Orloff?

Judith Orloff, MD, is the author of the bestseller *Positive Energy: 10 Extraordinary Prescriptions for Transforming Fatigue.* She is a practicing intuitive, a psychiatrist, and an assistant professor of psychiatry at UCLA, with a private practice in Los Angeles. Her other books are *Emotional Freedom, Second Sight,* and *Guide to Intuitive Healing.* She leads workshops on the interrelationship of intuition, energy, and medicine. She was a featured speaker at the Fortune Magazine's Most Powerful Women Summit. www.drjudithorloff.com.

FAVORITE BOOKS FOR JUDITH:

A Wrinkle in Time, Madeleine L'Engle
Stranger in a Strange Land, Robert Heinlein
House of Light, Mary Oliver
The Practice of the Presence of God, Brother Lawrence
The Unbearable Lightness of Being, Milan Kundera

JUDITH
ORLOFF

As a psychiatrist and intuitive, what I do isn't my job. It's my life's passion. With patients I listen with my intellect and my intuition, a potent inner wisdom that goes beyond the literal. For the world to move toward peace, sane decision-making, and empowered approaches to health and healing, intuition must be blended with the mind. Intuition is the language of the heart and allows us to see the material world as well as the Great Mystery all around us. Awaken to the small, still voice inside. Awaken to your inner self and the infinite grace that binds it to all sentient beings and to everything that has ever been and will be.

Who Is Sue Palmer?

A former head teacher in Scotland, Sue Palmer is well known to UK primary teachers through her courses on literacy, articles, and columns in the educational press. She has written hundreds of educational books and TV programs, and acts as a consultant to the Department for Education and Skills and the BBC. More recently she has written books for parents: *Toxic Childhood* as well as *Detoxing Childhood*. www.suepalmer.co.uk

BOOKS AND POEMS THAT HAVE CHANGED SUE'S LIFE:

Collected Essays and Reviews, William James
An Experiment in Education, Sybil Marshall
Children's Minds, Margaret Donaldson
"Song of a Man Who Has Come Through," D. H. Lawrence
"Ulysses," Alfred Lord Tennyson

SUE
PALMER

Children are the future. Tomorrow's world depends on what happens to children today. . . .

Babies need love, time, and personal attention, not incarceration in an institution. Children need first-hand experiences and time to learn from the real-life adults in their lives—not a sedentary, screen-based lifestyle at home and a test-driven pencil-and-paper regime at school. They need to play with their friends out in the real world, not just indoors on a machine. They need stories of courage, kindness, and honor, not images of vacuous celebrity, cruelty, and greed.

It takes a village to raise a child—can today's global electronic village rise to the challenge?

Who Is Gunter Pauli?

Gunter is an entrepreneur who has established ten companies and had ten books published in seventeen languages. He has also published thirty-six fables teaching science, emotions, and arts to children. He is the father of two sons and very happily married to his wife, Katherina. Gunter has been fortunate to dream one day about how we could regenerate the rainforest and put nature back on its thriving evolutionary path. Today, Gunter has helped restore a flourishing twenty-thousand-acre rainforest in Colombia and concluded that it only has just begun.

BOOKS THAT CHANGED GUNTER'S LIFE:

Mémoires d'Hadrien, Marguerite Yourcenar
Schachnovelle, Stefan Zweig
La Nuit, Elie Wiesel
Five Kingdoms, Lynn Margulis
Der Tod in Venedig, Thomas Mann

GUNTER
PAULI

We have to look at the world through the eyes of our children. They are the present, we are the past. If we only teach our children what we know, they can only do as badly as we are doing. We have to create the space so they can imagine solutions we cannot even dream of. The advantage is that children do not make a distinction between fantasy and reality. All is reality. Therefore, children can go for their dreams and make them happen. We cannot anymore. The dreams we need to make come true have to be big ones.

Who Is Anthony Peake?

Anthony Peake is a writer based near Liverpool, England. He is the author of two acclaimed books, *Is There Life after Death* and *The Daemon: A Guide to Your Extraordinary Secret Self.* These books introduce Anthony's paradigm-changing theory on consciousness and its relationship to the phenomenal world, a theory he calls Cheating the Ferryman. Anthony has a BA and a post-graduate qualification in management from the London School of Economics. He is a qualified psychometrician. Anthony is also a professional member of the International Association of Near-Death Studies (IANDS), the Scientific & Medical Network (SMN), and the Institute of Noetic Sciences (IONS). Anthony has made many radio and TV appearances across the UK, Europe, the United States, and Canada and has written articles for both popular and academic journals. He has also lectured across the UK and has presented his theory in New York. In July 2009 he was invited to be involved in a prestigious platform event at the National Theatre in London. www.anthonypeake.com

BOOKS THAT HAVE INSPIRED ANTHONY:

Wholeness and the Implicate Order, David Bohm

The Physics of Immortality, John Barrow and F. Tiper

The New Immortality, J. W. Dunne

A New Model of the Universe, P. D. Ouspensky

The Origin of Consciousness in the Breakdown of the Bicameral Mind, Julian Jaynes

ANTHONY
PEAKE

The magic of conscious experience is the greatest miracle and the deepest mystery in the known universe. Why should there be sentience rather than non-sentience? I genuinely believe that humanity will soon understand the ultimate nature of self-awareness, and in doing so, we will open up a whole new paradigm of understanding. The answers will be found within the deep structures of the brain and the counterintuitive world of particle physics. It is here that the observer creates the observed and the observed brings about the observer. My ultimate hope is that then we will finally understand that we are all just aspects of an ultimate wholeness, a divine singularity.

Who Is Judy Piatkus?

Judy Piatkus founded Piatkus Books in 1979. Over the years, it became one of England's leading independent publishing imprints. The company published a wide range of books, specializing in lifestyle and fiction titles and was a pioneer in bringing many ideas in the areas of personal development, self-help, and mind, body, and spirit to a global market. Judy Piatkus sold the company in 2007 and is now a keynote speaker. Under the name Judy Ashberg she has written *The Little Book of Women's Wisdom* and *Lovers' Wisdom.* www.judypiatkus.com

INFLUENTIAL BOOKS:

As a publisher of books in the area of spiritual and personal development, the books that have influenced my life have been too numerous to mention. However, *Living Magically* by Gill Edwards was the first book to open my mind to metaphysical concepts and ideas about energy and consciousness, and for that I shall always be very grateful.

JUDY
PIATKUS

I long for a time when every human being is free. No longer will anyone live in fear or slavery. Every human being shall recognize that we have all been created equal, that each one of us is a human soul entering the physical world in the same way, all of us wanting to live surrounded by peace, love, and harmony. We will reject all forms of war and violence, and we will learn to respect the differences between us and to work with those differences rather than against them. We shall all be free in every way—body, mind, and spirit.

Who Is Stuart Pimm?

Stuart Pimm is the Doris Duke Professor of Conservation Ecology at Duke University and winner of the 2006 Heineken Prize for Environmental Sciences. He documents the loss of the biodiversity—the variety of life—worldwide, but especially in the Everglades of Florida as well as Brazil and southern Africa. Most importantly, he seeks practical solutions to preventing extinction, whether those solutions require science, local development, changes in national policies, or a better understanding of ethical and religious issues. *The World According to Pimm: A Scientist Audits the Earth* is a critically acclaimed and optimistic book about the planet and what must be done to protect it.

BOOKS THAT HAVE INSPIRED STUART:

The World According to Pimm, Stuart Pimm

Population Studies of Birds, David Lambert Lack

Seven Pillars of Wisdom, T. E. Lawrence

Stability and Complexity in Model Ecosystems, Robert McCredie May

A Field Guide to the Birds of Britain and Europe, Roger T. Peterson, Guy Mountfort, and P. A. D. Hollum

STUART
PIMM

Pray that our children will not ask why we killed off lions and tigers and bears, and half of all creatures, great *and* small, whales and butterflies alike. For we are poised to do just that, diminishing the variety of life more massively in two generations than in all of human history. Children for all time will not understand why we were so careless. For we *can* act now to attend to the problems that beset our world, doing so with skill and passion, keeping it spectacularly beautiful, interesting, and diverse.

Who Is Tamzin Pinkerton?

Tamzin Pinkerton is the coauthor of *Local Food: How to Make It Happen in Your Community*, a book that features a variety of local food projects across the UK and beyond, with the hope of inspiring more of the same. She sees food as being a fun and magnetic starting point for change that can have profound consequences for the wider aims of community resilience. As a participant in the Transition Movement, Tamzin has been involved in community-based projects in Totnes, the country's first Transition Town. www.pinksprouts.org

FOUR BOOKS AND A SONG THAT HAVE INSPIRED TAMZIN:
Forest Gardening, Robert Adrian de Jauralde Hart
Healing With Whole Foods, Paul Pitchford
Commentaries on Living, Jiddu Krishnamurti
Animal, Vegetable, Miracle, Barbara Kingsolver
"Here Comes the Sun," The Beatles

TAMZIN
PINKERTON

As a species, we face a steep uphill struggle if we want to ensure life is preserved and enjoyed, in all its diversity, for generations to come. But if we see ourselves as powerless, overwhelmed victims of this precarious situation, then we will become sapped of our ability to climb the hill and make changes happen. We are, in fact, incredibly fortunate to be living at a time when our creativity and passions are crucially needed. They have to be and are being engaged, expressed, and directed toward the life-affirming, community-building, food-growing, Earth-respecting relationships that must be rebuilt. They also have to be rooted in the present—in today's actions, intentions, and decisions. Now is the time to be, love, create, and thrive, as we know we can.

Who Is Bill Plotkin?

Bill Plotkin has been a psychotherapist, research psychologist (studying dreams, meditation, hypnosis, and biofeedback), rock musician, river runner, professor of psychology, and mountain-bike racer. He is the founder of the Animas Valley Institute, which since 1980 has guided thousands of people through initiatory passages in nature. Currently an eco-therapist, depth psychologist, and wilderness guide, he leads a variety of experiential, nature-based, individuation programs. He is the author of *Soulcraft: Crossing into the Mysteries of Nature and Psyche* and *Nature and the Human Soul.* His doctorate in psychology is from the University of Colorado at Boulder. www.animas.org

BOOKS AND SONGS THAT HAVE MOST INSPIRED BILL'S LIFE:

The Dream of the Earth, Thomas Berry
Book of Hours, Rainer Maria Rilke
Memories, Dreams, Reflections, C. G. Jung
Joy of Man's Desiring, Jean Giono
The Dream and the Underworld, James Hillman
"Don't Go Back to Sleep," Jan Garrett

BILL
PLOTKIN

During the twenty-first century, the most radical evolutionary adventure ever to unfold on Earth is under way as we learn to shift human culture from a suicidal, life-destroying element to a creative eco-partnership worthy of both our extraordinary human potential and the Earth's dream for itself.

We must invent, or reinvent, a life-sustaining culture by a descent into the mysteries of psyche and nature, thereby recovering our native, mystical affiliation with the world, a revelatory experience available to everyone. The most potent seeds of cultural renaissance are the deeply imaginative ventures of those who have undergone this initiatory decent—mature artists and visionary leaders. They represent the future human that must now imagine—and create—for all earthly life.

Who Is John Pontin?

John Pontin, OBE, set up JT Design Build in 1961. Over a period of thirty-five years, the company developed a national profile, in particular for its stance on green issues in construction. John has a keen interest in sustainability. Apart from being the vice president of the Schumacher Society, he sits on the boards of Sustainability West, Business West, and the Royal Society of Arts Advisory Council. He was the chair of the Dartington Hall Trust from 1984 to 1997 and was a board member of the Natural Step (part of Forum for the Future). He was awarded an honorary doctor of laws by the University of Bristol in 2007, the same year that he founded the Converging World. www.theconvergingworld.org

BOOKS THAT HAVE INSPIRED JOHN'S THINKING AND PROJECTS:

Birth of the Chaordic Age, Dee Hock
The Natural Step Story, Karl-Henrik Robèrt
The Open Society and Its Enemies, Karl Popper
Creating a World without Poverty, Muhammad Yunus
Small Is Beautiful, E. F. Schumacher

JOHN PONTIN

Convergence is the underlying direction for the thousands of changes needed to deliver a better world. Our history is full of divergent processes that have created obscene inequalities, but it is in our power to alter our lives so that our economies, wealth, and well-being converge across and within nations to a level that the Earth can support—and we don't need to do this in isolation. By linking communities through the right forms of exchange, we can trade a way to a better, low-carbon life. The old model of just giving and forgetting must give way to new forms of investment, of social enterprises where proper business will make charity history.

Who Is Jonathon Porritt?

Jonathon Porritt is the founder and director of Forum for the Future and chairman of the UK Sustainable Development Commission (SDC), based in London. He is an eminent writer, broadcaster, and commentator on sustainable development. In 2000 Jonathon was appointed chairman of SDC by Tony Blair, prime minister of Britain. Porritt also represents several other organizations at the executive level, including the South-West Regional Development Agency, the Ashden Awards for Sustainable Energy, and the Prince of Wales's Business and Environmental Programme. Previous postings also include executive positions for Friends of the Earth, the Green Party, the National University of Distance Education (UNED), and World Wildlife Fund (WWF). His most recent book is *Capitalism as if the World Matters*. Jonathon received a CBE in 2000 for services to environmental protection. www.forumforthefuture.org.uk, www.sd-commission.org.uk

FIVE BOOKS THAT HAVE MOST INSPIRED JONATHON:

Small Is Beautiful, E. F. Schumacher
Silent Spring, Rachel Carson
The Limits to Growth, Dennis Meadows, Donella Meadows,
    and Jørgen Randers
The Upside of Down, Thomas Homer Dixon
Biomimicry, Janine Benyus

JONATHON
PORRITT

People do not understand the nature of the transition ahead of them—even now, as the shock of future climate change compels a "limited" transformation in conventional political and business attitudes. After two thousand years or more of driving forward a model of progress based on taming, subjugating, and improving "Nature," everything now depends on learning the art of cohabitation, of cocreating with Nature a shared and genuinely sustainable future. All else —equality, human rights, culture, religion, material progress, survival of the species, even—depends on that mindset evolution. Any vision for the future without that insight at its heart, however inspiring or progressive, can never be anything more than an illusion.

Who Is Sandra Postel?

Sandra Postel is one of the world's leading experts on international fresh water issues. Through research, writing, speaking, teaching, and consulting, she seeks to harmonize human activity with nature's life-supporting cycles of water. Among her books is the award-winning *Last Oasis*, the basis for a 1997 PBS television documentary; *Pillar of Sand: Can the Irrigation Miracle Last?;* and *Rivers for Life*, coauthored with Brian Richter. She is the recipient of two honorary doctor of science degrees, a Pew Scholars Award in Conservation and the Environment, and the *Scientific American* 50 award, for her contributions to water policy. Sandra directs the independent Global Water Policy Project and is a visiting senior lecturer at Mount Holyoke College.

FIVE BOOKS THAT INFLUENCED SANDRA'S LIFE:

Silent Spring, Rachel Carson
Composing a Life, Mary Catherine Bateson
Small Is Beautiful, by E. F. Schumacher
The Twenty-Ninth Day, Lester R. Brown
Refuge, Terry Tempest Williams

SANDRA
POSTEL

The challenges before us are less about healing the planet than about healing ourselves. We have so disconnected ourselves from Earth's beauty, mystery, and magic that we no longer feel whole. We seek satisfaction through material things, rather than through connection to communities. We have lost our sense of wonder, and our sense of place and belonging.

Here is an antidote: The tears we shed today—over war, death, disease, isolation, and aloneness—are comprised of molecules of water that have cycled through Earth's ecosystems for millennia. Let our tears connect us back to the beginning of life, and move us into constant joy at being alive.

Who Is John Randolph Price?

John Randolph Price, author of eighteen nonfiction books incorporating ancient wisdom and contemporary metaphysics, is the recipient of national and international awards for humanitarianism, progress toward global peace, and for contributions to a higher degree of positive living throughout the world.

He formed the Quartus Foundation for Spiritual Research in 1981 and serves as the chairman of the board. He is also the originator of World Healing Day, which began on December 31, 1986, with over five hundred million participants world-wide. The event has continued each year on the same date. www.quartus.org

FIVE BOOKS THAT HAVE SHAPED, INSPIRED, AND INFLUENCED JOHN'S LIFE:

The Secret Teachings of All Ages, Manly P. Hall
In Tune with the Infinite, Ralph Waldo Trine
Practicing the Presence, Joel Goldsmith
The Holographic Universe, Michael Talbot
Power through Constructive Thinking, Emmet Fox

JOHN RANDOLPH
PRICE

I have frequently been asked if we will ever achieve true peace on Earth. I believe we will—in that moment in time when peace comes forth in every mind, love flows forth from every heart, forgiveness reigns in every soul, and understanding becomes the common bond.

Could that possibly happen? Is it an unrealistic objective? Not if we truly believe that nothing is impossible. It all begins with each one of us individually—perhaps as a dream—and as the light of peace begins to shine from within, the dream becomes a reality.

That's my hope for the future.

Who Is Caroline Skelton Priebe?

Caroline Skelton Priebe founded the fashion label ULURU in Brooklyn, in July 2004, based on "slow fashion" design principles. She also cofounded the five-in-one designer retail collaborative in Williamsburg, Brooklyn, the hotbed of progressive American design and craft. In addition to operating and designing ULURU, Caroline is a stylist, image consultant, sustainable design and business model expert, and a certified Martha Beck life coach. She is currently writing a book titled *The Collection,* and an introduction to slow fashion, an investigation into garment communication and how building your personal collection can accurately speak your truth. www.ulurunyc.com, www.studio5in1.com, www.carolinepriebe.com

BOOKS THAT HAVE INFLUENCED CAROLINE:
Small Is Beautiful, E. F. Schumacher
The Omnivore's Dilemma, Michael Pollan
Developing Power, edited by Arvonne Fraser and Irene Tinker
Cradle to Cradle, William McDonough and Michael Braungart
The Four Agreements, Don Miguel Ruiz

CAROLINE
SKELTON
PRIEBE

We are at a point in history with a unique opportunity to create new sustainable economic models, businesses, and lives. I imagine an explosion of economic solutions where the powerful force of entrepreneurship is mobilized for eco-preservation and social enrichment. As part of the fashion community, I hope for increased awareness that we do not work in isolation—we are part of a process and aesthetics is only one part. Good design includes creating a production model where everyone in the process is nourished, including the Earth. Within this model, we might then deliver beautifully crafted garments that potentially serve a lifetime.

Who Is Dean Radin?

Dean Radin, PhD, earned degrees in electrical engineering (BSEE, MS) and psychology (PhD), the latter two from the University of Illinois, Champaign-Urbana. For over twenty years he has conducted research on the capacities of human consciousness through research appointments at Princeton University, University of Edinburgh, University of Nevada, SRI International, and the Institute of Noetic Sciences. Dean is the author of *The Conscious Universe*, *Entangled Minds*, dozens of book chapters, and hundreds of scientific and popular articles. He has served as president of the Parapsychological Association four times. www.ions.org

A FEW OF DEAN'S FAVORITE BOOKS:

Be Here Now, Ram Dass

Last and First Men, Olaf Stapledon

The Golem, Harry Collins and Trevor Pinch

Higher Creativity, Willis Harman and Howard Rheingold

The Spectrum of Consciousness, Ken Wilber

Quantum Reality, Nick Herbert

Journal of Scientific Exploration, Society for Scientific Exploration

DEAN
RADIN

Children of the world, keep asking the hard questions: Who are we? Why are we here? What is consciousness and what are its capacities? The truth is that we hardly understand anything about the universe, our existence, or what we're capable of. We're clever primates, just recently down from the trees, playing with dynamite and wondering what happens when we strike the fuse. Our exotic technologies, impressive scientific journals, and sober religious lore all sustain the illusion that someone, somewhere, must know what's going on. But it's not true. Not yet. Learn from your experiences, and keep asking the hard questions.

Who Is Carolyn Raffensperger?

Carolyn is the executive director of the Science and Environmental Health Network. In 1982 she left a career as an archaeologist in the desert to join the environmental movement. As an environmental lawyer she specializes in the fundamental changes in law and policy necessary for the protection and restoration of public health and the environment.

Carolyn is one of the best-known proponents of the precautionary principle. She coined the term "ecological medicine" to encompass the broad notions that both health and healing are entwined with the natural world. Carolyn is at the forefront of developing new models for government that depend on the larger ideas of precaution and ecological integrity. The new models include guardianship for future generations, a vision for the courts of the twenty-first century, and the public trust doctrine. www.sehn.org

BOOKS THAT HAVE INFLUENCED CAROLYN:

The Selected Poems of Wendell Berry
War and the Soul, Edward Tick
Listening to the Land, Derrick Jensen
A Chorus of Stones, Susan Griffin
A Sand County Almanac, Aldo Leopold

CAROLYN
RAFFENSPERGER

We each have a sacred and joyous responsibility to become ancestors of the future ones and leave an inheritance of a livable, beautiful planet as our legacy of love to those generations to come. Their world is in our hands. We are charged with living the Golden Rule toward the future beings of all species and treating them with compassion and generosity as we were treated. We can become guardians of future generations and make our legal, economic, and technological decisions with their well-being in mind. If we care for them wisely and compassionately, we will be called Beloved Ancestors.

Who Is Marcus Raskin?

Marcus Raskin is the cofounder and Distinguished Fellow of the Institute for Policy Studies in Washington, D.C. He served on President John F. Kennedy's Special Staff of the National Security Council, on the White House staff, and on the Presidential Panel on Educational Research and Development. After leaving government, Raskin was a leading antiwar activist, acquitted with Dr. Benjamin Spock and three others in the famous Boston 5 draft conspiracy case during the Indochina War. He is currently a professor of public policy at George Washington University and a member of the editorial board of *The Nation* magazine. His published works include numerous books on political theory, foreign policy, and national security, such as *Being and Doing*, *The Common Good*, *Visions and Revisions*, and *Liberalism*. Raskin's current work focuses on a ten-volume series on reconstruction and paths for the twenty-first century.

FIVE BOOKS OF INSPIRATION:

Intelligence in the Modern World, John Dewey, edited by Joseph Ratner
Civilization and its Discontents, Sigmund Freud
The Pentagon of Power, Lewis Mumford
Search for a Method, Jean-Paul Sartre
Black Reconstruction in America, W. E. B. DuBois

MARCUS
RASKIN

Visions without attention to material reality and specific practical moral action are of minimal value.

Imagination coupled to disciplined thought can change views of reality, as Einstein showed.

Projects and social inventions can widen the social space of freedom.

Who Is Sigrid Rausing?

Sigrid Rausing is the publisher of *Granta* magazine and, with her husband—film and theatre producer Eric Abraham—the joint proprietor of Granta Books and Portobello Books. She is also an anthropologist and has published *History, Memory and Identity in Post-Soviet Estonia,* as well as a range of scholarly articles in numerous journals. Sigrid had a two-year honorary fellowship at the Anthropology Department of University College, London following her PhD.

In 1995 she founded the Sigrid Rausing Trust, which funds projects and organizations in the areas of civil and political rights, women's rights, minority rights, and social and environmental justice. She has won three philanthropic awards, the International Service Human Rights Award, the Beacon Special Award for Philanthropy, and the Women's Funding Network's Changing Face of Philanthropy Award. Sigrid serves on the boards of Human Rights Watch in New York, the publishing company Atlantic UK, and Charleston, the former home of Vanessa Bell and Duncan Grant in Sussex. She is a governor of Sevenoaks School, UK.

WORKS THAT HAVE INFLUENCED SIGRID:

The Feminine Mystique, Betty Friedan
What Is the What, Dave Eggers
Scum of the Earth, Arthur Koestler
If Not Now, When?, Primo Levi
The Gulag Archipelago, Aleksandr Solzhenitsyn

SIGRID
RAUSING

I believe in human solidarity, in grassroots organizing, in feminism, and in human rights advocacy. There's hope in giving help, and there's hope in asking for help; that hope is baked into the fact that we are all humans and all essentially the same. We hold this truth to be self-evident, that all men are born equal.

Who Is William Rees?

William Rees is a human ecologist, ecological economist, professor and former director of the University of British Columbia's School of Community and Regional Planning (SCARP) in Vancouver, British Columbia. He is perhaps best known as the originator and codeveloper of "ecological footprint analysis." He has also authored 130 reviewed papers and book chapters, as well as numerous popular articles on humanity's (un)sustainability conundrum. The influence of Dr. Rees's work is widely recognized. He has lectured by invitation in twenty-five countries around the world. In 2006 he was elected to the Royal Society of Canada, and in 2007 he was awarded a prestigious Trudeau Foundation Fellowship.

BOOKS THAT HAVE STRONGLY INFLUENCED WILLIAM'S LIFE:

A Sand County Almanac, Aldo Leopold
The Selfish Gene, Richard Dawkins
Steady-State Economics, Herman E. Daly
Guns, Germs, and Steel, Jared Diamond
The Blank Slate, Steven Pinker

WILLIAM
REES

Homo sapiens is an unfinished work, a conflicted species endowed with high intelligence and self-awareness, but whose affairs are governed more by the crude iron of passion than the burnished gold of reason. To achieve sustainability, we must rise above base instinct to full human potential or else wink out ignominiously, a guttering candle in a violent storm of our own making. It would be a tragic paradox if, in the twenty-first century, this most technologically sophisticated of human societies succumbs yet again to the unconscious urgings of self-interested tribalism cloaked in defunct ideology. Our greatest hope lies in the ultimate triumph of enlightened reason over scripted determinism, whatever its source.

Who Is Judy Reeves?

Judy Reeves is a writer, teacher, and writing practice provocateur whose books include: *A Writer's Book of Days; Writing Alone, Writing Together; A Creative Writer's Kit;* and *The Writer's Retreat Kit.* Other works include two plays written with the Second Story Writers (a women's writing ensemble) and a chapbook of poetry, *The Kind of Woman She Is.* In addition to leading private writing workshops, Judy also teaches creative writing at the University of California, San Diego, and speaks at international writing conferences. She cofounded the Writing Center and is the executive director of San Diego Writers, Ink, a nonprofit arts organization. She lives and writes in San Diego, California. www.judyreeveswriter.com

BOOKS THAT HAVE INSPIRED JUDY:
Peace Is Every Step, Thich Nhat Hanh
Love Is Letting Go of Fear, Gerald Jampolsky
Alcoholics Anonymous, AA World Services
The Writing Life, Annie Dillard
If You Want to Write, Brenda Ueland

JUDY
REEVES

I believe that each and every human being has a need to express themselves creatively, and that each of us has been given a gift of self-expression that is creative and unique to us. A companion belief I hold is that each of us has a responsibility to use our gifts for the betterment of all. This is how we evolve, with each of us giving back in our own original and creative way. Our contribution to the whole raises all of us to a higher level and without our creative expression, we would, as a species, become extinct.

Who Is Fiona Reynolds?

Fiona, forty-eight, has been the director-general of the National Trust for England, Wales, and Northern Ireland since 2001. The Trust is one of the world's most fascinating and effective charities, fulfilling its responsibilities to "look after special places for ever, for everyone" through the ownership of six hundred fifty thousand acres of land, seven hundred-plus miles of coastline, and over two hundred fifty great houses and their gardens and parks. Before arriving at the Trust, Fiona had a long career in the voluntary conservation movement with the Council for National Parks and the Consortium for Policy Research in Education, as well as a short, somewhat counterintuitive spell in the Cabinet Office as director of the Women's Unit. Fiona is married, has three daughters, and lives in a small village near Cirencester among chickens, ducks, cats, and vegetables. Fiona loves walking, landscape history, classical music/opera, and reading.

THE BOOK THAT HAS MOST INSPIRED FIONA:
The Making of the English Landscape, W. G. Hoskins

FIONA
REYNOLDS

I take my inspiration from the founders of the National Trust—Hill, Rawnsley, and Hunter, true pioneers and Victorian radicals. Unhappy with the way industrialization was changing the face of our country, they were determined to stand up for beauty and the chance for everyone to experience it. My vision is a world where countryside, wildlife, and cultural heritage are protected for future generations to enjoy. It's about cherishing the things that really matter—fresh air, open spaces, beauty, tranquility, and history—and fighting for their protection against the ravages of climate change and pollution. My vision also encompasses integrity in farming and food production: the choices we, as consumers, make about the food we eat and the lives we live fundamentally impact our quality of life.

Who Is Cheryl Richardson?

Cheryl Richardson is the author of *The New York Times* bestselling books *Take Time for Your Life, Life Makeovers, Stand Up for Your Life,* and *The Unmistakable Touch of Grace.* Richardson was the first president of the International Coach Federation and holds one of their first Master Certified Coach credentials. Her work has been covered widely in the media, including *The Today Show, Good Morning America, The New York Times, Good Housekeeping,* and *O* magazine. Richardson was the team leader for the Lifestyle Makeover series on *The Oprah Winfrey Show,* and she accompanied Winfrey on the Live Your Best Life tour. She writes a column for *Body + Soul* magazine, conducts an Internet talk radio show on Hay House Radio, and hosts an international community online. www.hayhouseradio.com, www.cherylrichardson.com

BOOKS THAT HAVE INSPIRED CHERYL:

Unlimited Power, by Anthony Robbins
Power vs. Force, David Hawkins
The Sermon on the Mount, Emmet Fox
The Bhagavad Gita, translated by Paramahansa Yogananda

CHERYL
RICHARDSON

Experience has taught me that the greatest gift I can give to humanity is my ongoing commitment to raise my level of consciousness. The more conscious I become, the greater my desire to protect the environment, to be an advocate for those without a voice—animals, children, or the less fortunate—and the more powerful my need to maintain a level of optimism and belief in our collective good, which will ultimately save us from destruction. To make choices that elevate consciousness on the planet—now that's visionary.

Who Is John Robbins?

John Robbins is the author of six international bestsellers, including *Diet for a New America,* and *The Food Revolution.* The only son of the founder of the Baskin-Robbins ice cream empire, John was groomed to follow in his father's footsteps, but chose to walk away from Baskin-Robbins and the immense wealth it represented so he could "pursue the deeper American Dream … the dream of a society at peace with its conscience because it respects and lives in harmony with all life forms. A dream of a society that is truly healthy, practicing a wise and compassionate stewardship of a balanced ecosystem."

Considered to be one of the most eloquent and powerful spokespersons for a sane, ethical, and sustainable future, John is the founder and board chair emeritus of EarthSave International and board chair emeritus of Yes! He is the recipient of many awards, including the Rachel Carson Award, the Albert Schweitzer Humanitarian Award, and the Peace Abbey's Courage of Conscience Award. www.earthsave.org, www.yesworld.org

FIVE BOOKS THAT HAVE INSPIRED JOHN:
The Chalice and the Blade, Riane Eisler
Diet for a New America, John Robbins
A Woman's Worth, Marianne Williamson
The Sacred Balance, David Suzuki
Silent Spring, Rachel Carson

JOHN
ROBBINS

I believe that the real news on this planet is love—why it exists, where it came from, and where it is going. I believe that ultimately it is the love in our lives that underlies and makes possible our greatest healing and longevity. Whether we acknowledge it or not, we all have a choice to be either accomplices in the status quo or everyday revolutionaries. We have a choice whether to succumb to the cultural trance, eat fast food, and race by each other in the night, or to build lives of caring, substance, and healing. So much depends on that choice.

Who Is Belvie Rooks?

Belvie Rooks is a writer, educator, and producer whose work weaves the worlds of spirituality, feminism, ecology, racial and environmental justice, and a passion for dialogue. She is a board member of both the Institute of Noetic Sciences (IONS) and the Ella Baker Center, and formerly sat on the board of Bioneers. Belvie is the executive producer of *Watts Up! Exploring the Frontiers of Consciousness*, featuring Edgar Mitchell, Lynne Twist, Archbishop Desmond Tutu, and other global visionaries. Ms. Rooks is the producer and host of *ConverZations that Matter*, which looks deeply at the larger questions of race, cosmology, and consciousness. www.wattsupjourney.com, www.shiftinaction.com

FIVE BOOKS THAT HAVE HELPED TO SHAPE BELVIE'S VISION:
The Man Who Talks with the Flowers, Glenn Clark
The Universe Story, Brian Swimme
Race and the Cosmos, Barbara Holmes
The Way of the Explorer, Edgar Mitchell
KMT: In the House of Life, Ayi Kwei Armah

BELVIE
ROOKS

One of my grandmother's most instructive sayings during hard times came from the Book of Esther: "But for such a time as this that you were born." During times such as this, when the ice caps are melting; when, in their despair and hopelessness, some of our children are killing each other while others kill themselves; my grandmother's voice is a persistent presence: "But for such a time as this that you were born."

In the grand orchestration of hope and possibility for our children and the planet, we have each, indeed, chosen this moment to answer the sacred calling.

Who Is David Roth?

Singer, songwriter, recording artist, and community builder, David Roth strikes many chords, hearts, and minds with his unique songs, moving stories, offbeat observations, and powerful singing and subject matter. David has taken his music, experience, and expertise to a wide variety of venues in this and other countries over the last two decades, and his work has found its way to Carnegie Hall; the United Nations; several Chicken Soup for the Soul books; Peter, Paul and Mary concerts; NASA's Goddard Space Center; and ten recordings on the Wind River and Stockfisch labels. Lately David has been teaching singing, songwriting, and performance at music camps across North America, helping people of all ages and levels meaningfully reconnect with music in their lives. www.davidrothmusic.com

FIVE BOOKS THAT DAVID STILL ENJOYS READING:

Autobiography of a Yogi, Paramahansa Yogananda
Three Cups of Tea, Greg Mortenson and David Oliver Relin
A Soprano on Her Head, Eloise Ristad
Talking on the Water, Jonathan White
Songwriters on Songwriting, Paul Zollo

DAVID
ROTH

Reuse bags everywhere you go. Eat less meat. Grow something edible in your yard. Buy organic. Buy local. Walk, hike, jog, bike, skate, ski, roll, float, carpool, use public transportation, and less car whenever possible. Recycle everything you can, even things you never thought of recycling before. Support small businesses. Sing every day, especially if you think you can't. Exercise. Get enough sleep. Drink lots of water. Less TV. Read. Know your neighbors. When you disagree with someone, entertain their point of view for a few moments. Use words carefully. Listen to your body. Be kind. Volunteer. Encourage. Give thanks.

Who Is Peter Russell?

Peter Russell, MA, DCS, is the author of ten books and producer of two award-winning videos. His work integrates Eastern and Western understandings of the mind, exploring their relevance to the world today and to humanity's future. He was one of the first people to introduce human potential seminars into the corporate field, and for twenty years worked with major corporations on creativity, learning methods, stress management, and personal development. His books include *Waking Up in Time* and most recently *From Science to God*. www.peterrussell.com

SIGNIFICANT BOOKS IN PETER'S LIFE:

Impersonal Life, anonymous

E.T. 101, Diana Luppi, Zoev Jho, Brandt Morgan, and James Finnell

Lost in the Cosmos, Walker Percy

The Atman Project, Ken Wilber

A Course in Miracles, Foundation for Inner Peace

PETER
RUSSELL

Throughout human history, some people have awoken to the true nature of consciousness. We call them the "enlightened ones"—the mystics, seers, saints, rishis, roshis, lamas—the wise ones who have liberated themselves from petty human foibles. In the past, such people were few and far between. Today, countless people across the planet are actively treading this path, learning from each other and those who have gone before—rediscovering for themselves the timeless wisdom that will allow us to navigate our way safely through these troubled times. They are our greatest hope.

Who Is Tim Rylands?

Tim Rylands has been a primary school teacher for over twenty years. He has been described as an extremely gifted and inspirational teacher, someone who is passionately devoted to using the creative potential of technology to foster communication and literacy skills amongst children. Tim's magical ability to inspire children, through the power of new technology and visual worlds, is both innovative and refreshing. He has pioneered inspirational teaching methods that motivate pupils to all new levels of achievement. In 2005 Tim was honored with the BECTA ICT Award, one of the highest creative teaching awards throughout the UK. Now working as an independent teacher and adviser, Tim facilitates and shares his extensive knowledge with schools, governmental organizations, and private institutions around the world. www.timrylands.com

A SONG THAT HAS DEEPLY INSPIRED TIM'S LIFE:
"The Living Years," Mike and the Mechanics

TIM
RYLANDS

The word "teacher" is too one-sided.

In this goal-driven age, we could think that education is imparting a body of knowledge, rather than a shared journey of discovery. Fascination is a tool that can be easily neglected. This digital age brings such potential for communication. Our species will survive from a sharing of understanding. We need to inspire young people and fire their imaginations; enhance their creativity and confidence, so they can pick ideas up and start to juggle with them; encourage resourcefulness through challenge, but also the ability to reflect, change, and benefit from the experience of others; and motivate a love of learning for life.

Who Is Wolfgang Sachs?

Wolfgang Sachs is a researcher, university teacher, and author. He heads research on globalization and sustainability at the Wuppertal Institute for Climate, Environment, and Energy in Germany. He is an honorary professor at Kassel University and regular lecturer at Schumacher College, England, and is also a member of the Club of Rome. His has become known as the editor of the widely read *Development Dictionary: A Guide to Knowledge as Power*. His most recent book is *Fair Future: Resource Conflicts, Security, and Global Justice*. www.wupperinst.org

BOOKS THAT CHANGED WOLFGANG'S LIFE:

Tools for Conviviality, Ivan Illich
Small Is Beautiful, E. F. Schumacher
The Great Transformation, Karl Polanyi

WOLFGANG SACHS

Beyond a threshold, things become thieves of time. Goods need to be selected, bought, set up, used, experienced, maintained, tidied away, dusted, repaired, stored, and disposed of. Even the most beautiful of objects and the most valuable of interactions gnaw away at our time—the most restricted of all resources. As a consequence, we have become poorer in time as we became richer in things. Scarcity of time has thus turned out to be the nemesis of affluence. Yet the full value of things can only be enjoyed when they are given attention: they have to be properly used, adequately enjoyed, and carefully cultivated. So poverty of time degrades the richness of goods. Frugality, therefore, is a key to well-being.

Who Is Elisabet Sahtouris?

Elisabet Sahtouris is a Greek-American evolution biologist, futurist, business consultant, event organizer, and UN consultant on indigenous peoples. She is a popular lecturer, television and radio personality, author of *EarthDance* and *Biology Revisioned*, and coauthor of *A Walk through Time: From Stardust to Us*. She was a participant in the Humanity 3000 dialogues of the Foundation for the Future and the Synthesis Dialogues with the Dalai Lama in Dharamsala. She consults with corporations and government organizations in Australia, Brazil, and the United States. She promotes a vision she believes will result in the sustainable health and well-being of humanity within the larger living systems of Earth and the cosmos.

WORKS THAT HAVE INSPIRED ELISABET:

Language, Thought, and Reality, Benjamin Lee Whorf,
   edited by John Bissell Carroll
The Self-Organizing Universe, Erich Jantsch
The "Unknown" Reality, Jane Roberts
Adventures in Kinship with all Life, J. Allen Boone
Gaia, James Lovelock

ELISABET
SAHTOURIS

As an evolution biologist, I know humanity is scheduled to evolve now from juvenile competition to mature cooperation, as have so many species before us. It's happening as young adults on the Internet, the first generation in history with the power of global conversation, show no interest in racism, greed, or war, but rather in creating, caring, giving, and sharing. They don't need to clean up our mess; they can simply create the world they want, making pacts not to kill each other, surfing the waves of climate change by building cooperative economies, inventing sustainable technologies, and greening deserts to weave global community. They inspire me!

Who Are Masami and Hiroo Saionji?

Masami Saionji is a spiritual leader respected in Japan and internationally. She and her husband, Hiroo, are chairperson and president, respectively, of the Goi Peace Foundation, a peace-building educational NGO based in Tokyo, and the New York–based World Peace Prayer Society, which is dedicated to spreading the universal prayer "May Peace Prevail on Earth." Together they travel the world to inspire awareness of peace and to build a transdisciplinary network for creating a new civilization.

Masami Saionji's books include *The Golden Key to Happiness*, *You Are the Universe,* and *Vision for the 21st Century*. www.goipeace.or.jp, www.worldpeace.org

BOOKS THAT HAVE INSPIRED MASAMI AND HIROO SAIONJI:

God and Man, Masahisa Goi

Science and the Akashic Field, Ervin Laszlo

Le Trésor des Humbles, Maurice Maeterlinck

The God Delusion, Richard Dawkins

The Divine Code of Life, Kazuo Murakami

MASAMI &
HIROO
SAIONJI

Since ancient times, the Japanese people believed in *Kotodama*—the spirit of words.

Words have the power to create and inspire.
Words have magical energy that ripples out into the world.
Every one of us is free to choose the words we use.
Our own words can invite happiness or misfortune, hope or despair.
They can enliven or kill, create peace or make war.
It is neither governments nor learned people that will guide humanity in the twenty-first century. It is the daily words of each individual that will create a bright future for our planet.

May Peace Prevail on Earth.

Who Is Marilyn Mandala Schlitz?

Marilyn Mandala Schlitz, PhD, is a clinical research scientist, medical anthropologist, writer, speaker, and change consultant. Her work over the past three decades explores the interface of consciousness, science, and healing. She has published hundreds of articles on consciousness studies in scholarly and popular journals and has lectured widely on a number of topics, including talks at the United Nations, the Smithsonian Institution, the Explorers Club, and Harvard Medical School. She has taught at Trinity and Stanford universities, and currently serves on the editorial boards of the *Permanente Journal* and *Explore: The Journal of Science and Healing*. She is the vice president for Research and Education at the Institute of Noetic Sciences, senior scientist at the California Pacific Medical Center, and chief learning officer at Integral Learning Corporation. Marilyn possesses a rare ability to translate complex ideas into a common-sense language that excites our imaginations. Her books include *Consciousness & Healing: Integral Approaches to Mind-Body Medicine* and *Living Deeply: The Art and Science of Transformation in Everyday Life*.

FIVE OF MARILYN'S FAVORITE BOOKS:

The Structure of Scientific Revolutions, Thomas Kuhn
Mind and Nature, Gregory Bateson
Global Mind Change, Willis Harman
In Over Our Heads, Robert Kegan
A Mapmaker's Dream, James Cowan

MARILYN
MANDALA
SCHLITZ

Our times call upon us to stand witness to hope. It is so easy to find causes for despair. And yet we will remain stuck, individually and socially, if we can't find the inspiration to move toward a more sustainable vision for humanity. We are meaning-making creatures. Within our consciousness is the root cause of many of our problems—and their solutions. We can choose how we direct our awareness and how we respond to the world in which we live. Each of us carries within us opportunities to help craft new meaning systems for the twenty-first century that can nurture life in all its forms for generations to come. This is indeed hopeful.

Who Is Diana Schumacher?

In 1979 Diana Schumacher, together with her husband, set up Schumacher Projects Partnership, a management and environmental consultancy. She is also a director for Work Structuring Limited, a company founded by Christian Schumacher, which focuses on organizational renewal and the creation of "whole" work systems. She has been an active member of the environmental movement since the 1970s and serves on the executive council of over twenty-five organizations, including the Environmental Law Foundation, which she cofounded in 1991. www.work-structuring.com

FIVE BOOKS THAT HAVE INFLUENCED DIANA:

A Guide for the Perplexed, E. F. Schumacher

The Educational Philosophy of Mahatma Gandhi, M. S. Patel

May They All Be One, Chiara Lubich

The Betrothed, Alessandro Manzoni

No Man Is an Island, Thomas Merton

DIANA
SCHUMACHER

We all like to think of ourselves as loving people. However, there is still much work to be done on the inner level of consciousness before we can play a fuller part in the great work of transformation. Anyone who has narrowly escaped death or appears to be *living on borrowed time* appreciates the beauty and immense opportunity of each present moment in which we still have time to love.

The challenge is to be the *first to love and to love universally in every situation,* including loving those who hurt us, for whatever reason. The challenge is also to look at all the faults, defects, and insults as a wonderful opportunity to love more, and to go beyond ourselves with the *generosity of love.* We may come to look at each negative situation as a personal gift for us and an opportunity to perfect our own love.

Who Is Beverly Schwartz?

Beverly Schwartz is a behavioral scientist and social marketing specialist who uses marketing to change social behaviors. She has worked on multiple large-scale national health campaigns since she helped write and pass the Minnesota Clean Indoor Air Act, America's first statewide law to ban smoking in all public places. She helped develop and manage the America Responds to Aids campaign for the U.S. Centers for Disease Control and Prevention, the National Eye Care Project for the Academy of Ophthalmology, and the Youth Anti-Drug Media Campaign for the Executive Office of the White House. For the past ten years, she was an associate editor of *Social Marketing Quarterly* and is currently vice president for Global Marketing at Ashoka, the largest community of social entrepreneurs in the world.

WORKS THAT HAVE DEEPLY IMPACTED BEVERLY'S LIFE:

Man's Search for Meaning, Viktor Frankl
Blackberry Winter, Margaret Mead
George Sand, Curtis Cate
Ivanhoe, Sir Walter Scott

TWO BOOKS THAT BEVERLY ALWAYS WISHED WOULD HAVE IMPACTED HER LIFE:

A La Recherche du Temps Perdu, Marcel Proust
The Fountainhead, Ayn Rand

BEVERLY
SCHWARTZ

I absolutely insist on having at least one good laugh a day. The laugh must bubble up from my belly and be audible—primarily to myself. Laughing inwardly at the small things that most people may find commonplace makes me feel as if the universe and I are playing with each other and sharing secrets. Having the ability to laugh with myself keeps me light, authentic, and empathetic. It makes me feel that as long as the people around me and I have laughter, we have life. On a day when I deal with sadness or witness life's cruelty to others, laughter keeps me going, laughter keeps me whole, laughter makes me feel that the world can one day heal itself.

Who Is Gary E. Schwartz?

Gary E. Schwartz, PhD, is a professor of psychology, medicine, neurology, psychiatry, and surgery as well as the director of the Laboratory for Advances in Consciousness and Health at the University of Arizona. He is also the corporate director of development of energy healing at Canyon Ranch. His books focus on the integration of science, spirituality, and healing, and include *The Afterlife Experiments: Breakthrough Scientific Evidence of Life after Death, The G.O.D. Experiments: How Science Is Discovering God in Everything, Including Us,* and *The Energy Healing Experiments: Science Reveals Our Natural Power to Heal.* He has taught at Harvard and Yale universities. His pioneering and award-winning research has been featured in numerous documentaries. www.drgaryschwartz.com, www.lach.web.arizona.edu

BOOKS THAT HAVE INSPIRED SCHWARTZ:

Reason to Hope, Ralph Wayne Kraft

The Anatomy of Reality, Jonas Salk

Living Systems, James G. Miller

Passport to the Cosmos, John E. Mack

Code Name God, Mani Bhaumik

GARY E. SCHWARTZ

Imagine that science is on the verge of verifying the existence of a spiritual reality that extends all the way from our individually experienced conscious minds to a Universal Mind of infinite intelligence, compassion, and wisdom.

Imagine that science is on the verge of revealing our innate capacity for communicating with—and manifesting—this Consciousness Potential for the survival, health, and evolution of everything, including us.

Imagine that science and spirituality are coming together again, and in the process not only integrating and honoring our species history—and learning from it—but extending and awakening our individual and collective Awareness Potential for fostering healing, peace, and transformation.

Einstein said, "Imagination is more important than knowledge." If ever there was a Reason to Hope for the evolution and transformation of our imagination, it is now.

Who Is Ruth Sewell?

Ruth is a teacher, psychotherapist, and clincial and academic supervisor. Over twenty-five years, her professional work has been principally focused on supporting people whose lives are affected by cancer; the integration of holistic approaches to treating illness; and the significant interplay between health, illness, spirituality, and the environment. She is committed to raising the importance of care, support, and education of health care practitioners, which includes helping them to identify not only how they can improve their professional work with colleagues and clients, by coming from a place of heart-centered and soulful care, but also how they can remain mindful and committed to their own self-care and well-being. www.ruthsewell.co.uk

BOOKS THAT INSPIRED RUTH'S LIFE:

Evening Thoughts, Thomas Berry

Consciousness and Healing, edited by Marilyn Schlitz,
   Tina Amorok, and Marc Micozzi

Reinvention of Work, Matthew Fox

Shadows of the Sacred, Frances Vaughan

Ecopsycology, edited by Theodore Roszak, Mary Gomes, and Allen Kanner

RUTH
SEWELL

My vision is for a renewal of awareness and an enduring reconnection amongst all people to the sacredness of the World. That humans will be sensitive not only to the needs of the Earth but to the magnificent biodiversity of life so that a harmonious and mutually sustaining wider world community can be experienced. That every day each one of us can experience a sense of wonder and awe about this life. I hope we can reverse the intensity and isolation of individualism and self-centeredness so that we can cocreate and experience the enrichment and healing that being part of the greater whole has to offer.

Who Is Robert Shetterly?

Originating from Ohio, Robert Shetterly is the universally known artist of Americans Who Tell the Truth, a nationwide portrait exhibition that has been touring the States for several years. Shetterly's collection of over one hundred portraits depicts American truth-tellers from past and present. The exhibitions are nonpolitical and are displayed at various churches, schools, and universities across the country. Shetterly is a self-taught artist, and his work has been used by numerous newspapers and in over thirty books. He is also widely known for his painted etchings based on William Blake's *Proverbs of Hell*. His painting has tended toward the narrative and the surreal, and he has not been, until recently, a portrait painter. www.americanswhotellthetruth.org

WORKS THAT HAVE GREATLY INSPIRED ROBERT:

Credo, William Sloane Coffin

The Poems of Mary Oliver

"A Time to Break Silence," speech by Martin Luther King, Jr., April 4, 1967

The Photographs of Dorothea Lange

A People's History of the United States, Howard Zinn

ROBERT
SHETTERLY

The struggle of the twenty-first century will be between those who think they can create reality with power and violence and exploitation, and those who accept the essential reality that nature controls our fate. Some of us are sawing through the fragile limb on which we perch in the universe, and some are wondering why those with the saw love death more than life. Human, plant, and animal life on the planet is not so much being endangered by too many poor people as by very few people wanting too much.

Who Is Andrew Simms?

Andrew Simms is the policy director and head of the Climate Change Programme at the New Economics Foundation (NEF), the award-winning UK think-and-do tank. He is the author of numerous publications, including the books *Ecological Debt: The Health of the Planet and the Wealth of Nations*, and *Tescopoly: How One Shop Came Out on Top and Why It Matters,* and coeditor of *Do Good Lives Have to Cost the Earth?* He studied at the London School of Economics and for several years was a researcher and advocate for international development charities such as Oxfam and Christian Aid. He was one of the original campaigners for the Jubilee 2000 debt relief movement. He is a board member of Greenpeace UK and The Energy and Resources Institute (TERI) Europe, an associate editor of *Resurgence* magazine, and a regular contributor to the national press and broadcast media. He lives in London with his family and bicycle. www.neweconomics.org

FIVE OF ANDREW'S FAVORITE BOOKS:
All That Is Solid Melts into Air, Marshall Berman
Late Victorian Holocausts, Mike Davis
The Great Crash, 1929, John Kenneth Galbraith
Galápagos, Kurt Vonnegut
Passage to Juneau, Jonathan Raban

ANDREW
SIMMS

Imagine what if, after all, we are the only way that the universe can know itself.

As far as we know, we are alone to bear witness with our unlikely gift of human consciousness.

Like priests left to gaze upon and protect a sacred, life-giving flame, we might think twice before sneezing.

Being alive today, with all our flaws and staggering potential, we have won a competition in space, time, and place that has far, far longer odds than any national lottery.

Before we tear up our ticket, my hope is that we have the mindfulness to realize the meaning and beauty of our win.

Then, we will celebrate, and organize life like a party at which everyone gets enough to eat and drink, room on the dance floor, a roof over their heads, and a sky clear enough to see the stars.

Finally, to keep the good times rolling, we will be careful, as we party, not to burn the house down.

Who Is Nina Simons?

Nina Simons, a social entrepreneur, is the co-executive director of Bioneers and has coproduced the Bioneers Conference since 1990. She previously served as the president of Seeds of Change and as director of strategic marketing for Odwalla. In 2002 she produced UnReasonable Women for the Earth, a retreat for diverse women leaders and an incubator that helped stimulate the formation of CodePink: Women for Peace. Nina speaks and teaches nationally and internationally about women's leadership, cultivating relational intelligence, and organizations as living systems. www.bioneers.org

NINA'S MOST INSPIRATIONAL BOOKS AND FILMS:

The Burning Times (video/dvd about the Hidden Holocaust of Women)

A New Earth, Eckhart Tolle

Centering in Pottery, Poetry and the Person, M. C. Richards

An Unspoken Hunger, Terry Tempest Williams

Daughters of Copper Woman, Anne Cameron

Human Purpose and the Field of the Future, Peter Senge, Joseph Jaworski, C. Otto Scharmer, and Betty Sue Flowers

NINA
SIMONS

Reconnecting With Our Relations Throughout the Web of Life

This era asks that we listen, closely, to all our ways of knowing. Our dreams inform us from the unseen world, connecting us to the mystery. Our hearts connect us to the world of feeling, of relationships. Our bellies inform us when something unjust is happening, birthing a roar of outrage when needed. Our hands know to act, in correct response to the imbalances we perceive. Our minds offer us the ability to analyze, but must learn to speak in harmony with the rest. Externally, it's vital to cultivate our empathic connection to place, to each other, to animals, to the spirit of the natural world. It is only by nourishing our ability to stay connected to the whole of who we are, that we'll respond with love, compassion, and fierce dignity to the transformations and violence around us.

Who Is John St. Augustine?

John St. Augustine is an American producer and radio broadcaster who has scooped numerous awards for his informative and inspirational talk radio shows. A radio veteran, he has broadcast over seventy-five hundred programs and interviewed more than five thousand guests. John is widely recognized as the creator of the much acclaimed and syndicated *Powerthoughts*—one-minute uplifting and thought-provoking vignettes that air across America. Since 2006, John has produced the Oprah & Friends channel for XM Satellite Radio. As a much-sought-after speaker and communicator on human potential, John has delivered keynote presentations to over half a million people. In 2006 John published his book, *Living an Uncommon Life: Essential Lessons from 21 Extraordinary People.* Married with two children, he now divides his time between Michigan and Chicago. www.johnstaugustine.com

BOOKS AND SONGS THAT HAVE INSPIRED JOHN:

Life and Teaching of the Masters of the Far East, Baird T. Spalding
Self-Reliance and Other Essays, Ralph Waldo Emerson
The Power of Your Subconscious Mind, Joseph Murphy
Mutant Message Down Under, Marlo Morgan
The Strenuous Life, President Theodore Roosevelt
"Rocky Mountain High," John Denver
"One of Us," Joan Osborne

JOHN ST.
AUGUSTINE

The most powerful gift available to the human species is our voice—it is the medium that allows us to give vibration to the thoughts we think, thus bringing them into existence. This incredible instrument can hold the attention of millions through spoken word and song—for it is the very sound of our soul. The utterance of one simple word can make or break the human spirit. Every single voice is a soloist that makes up the world choir, and—if tuned to the highest vibration—the human voice in its divine resonance becomes the healing music of the universe.

Who Is Brother David Steindl-Rast?

Born in Vienna, Austria, David Steindl-Rast studied art, anthropology, and psychology at the Vienna Academy of Fine Arts, where he received his MA, and earned a PhD from the University of Vienna. In 1953 he joined Mount Saviour Benedictine Monastery, where he is now a senior member. He began studying Zen in the 1960s and became a pioneer in interfaith dialogue. In 1975 he received the Martin Buber Award for his achievements building bridges between religious traditions. His books include *Gratefulness, The Heart of Prayer; A Listening Heart*; and *Belonging to the Universe* (with Fritjof Capra). Currently, Brother David serves as the founding adviser of the Gratefulness organization. www.gratefulness.org

BOOKS AND POEMS THAT ARE IMPORTANT TO BROTHER DAVID'S LIFE:

The Power of Now, Eckhart Tolle
Jesus Today, Albert Nolan
Integral Spirituality, Ken Wilber
Letters to a Young Poet, Rainer Maria Rilke
Four Quartets, T. S. Eliot
Sonnets to Orpheus, Rainer Maria Rilke
"The Mountain," W. S. Merwin
"Singapore," Mary Oliver

BROTHER **DAVID** STEINDL-RAST

Every moment is a *given* moment; the appropriate response is gratefulness. The gift within every gift is opportunity; grateful people use this gift creatively. Grateful living has power to heal our lives and our world. Research shows: grateful people are happier and healthier. What we take for granted leaves us cold; gratefulness sparks joy. Grateful for what we have, we need less and can share more. Grateful to Mother Earth, we take better care of her gifts.

A wellspring of gratefulness in every heart waits to be tapped; once it flows, the whole Earth flowers like a well-watered garden.

Who Is Malcolm Stern?

Malcolm Stern is a group and individual psychotherapist with twenty years of experience. He was a cofounder of Alternatives, the multidisciplinary lecture series at St. James Church in London, and runs groups internationally. His book on relationships, *Falling in Love, Staying in Love,* was published in 2004. He was a copresenter of Channel 4's British series on relationships, *Made for Each Other,* in 2004 and 2005. www.malcolmstern.com

BOOKS THAT HAVE INSPIRED MALCOLM:

Everything by Hermann Hesse, especially *Narziss and
    Goldmund, Siddhartha,* and *The Glass Bead Game*
Island, Aldous Huxley
Man's Search for Meaning, Viktor Frankl
How Can I help?, Ram Dass and Paul Gorman
Meetings at the Edge, Stephen Levine
The Psychology of Romantic Love, Robert A. Johnson

MALCOLM
STERN

We are living in a time of opportunity. Life as we know it will change dramatically. Rather than a time for heroes, this is a time for cocreation. We are called to evolve into what we can become, and the tools we have to find are love, intimacy, and the willingness to be authentic. We not only have a need but a duty to find others of like mind to offer mutual support and friendship in this evolutionary journey.

Who Is Tessa Tennant?

Tessa Tennant is the executive chair and cofounder of the Ice Organisation, a personal carbon management and loyalty program. Tessa cofounded the UK's first equity investment fund for sustainable development in 1988. She was the chair and cofounder of the UK Social Investment Forum and of the Carbon Disclosure Project. In 2001 she cofounded and was the first chair of the Association for Sustainable and Responsible Investment in Asia (ASrIA), based in Hong Kong. She remains on the board. She is a board member of the Calvert Social Funds in Washington, D.C. She serves on the jury panel of the FT-IFC Sustainable Banking Awards. In 2003 she received the Sustainability Leadership Award by SAM/SPG of Switzerland and in 2004 was a joint winner of the City of Goteborg International Environmental Leadership Prize. She is a Schumacher Fellow, a World Wildlife Fund (WWF) UK ambassador, and winner of the 2001 Media Natura Environmental Awarenesss Award, UK.

BOOKS THAT HAVE INSPIRED TESSA:

News from Nowhere, William Morris
The Ecology of Commerce, Paul Hawken
Biomimicry, Janine Benyus
Atlases

TESSA
TENNANT

Who could have imagined twenty years ago that in 2008 investment into clean-tech would be one of the fastest growing categories of start-up financing? It gives me great hope for what we might achieve in the next crucial twenty years. My experience makes me defiant toward those who say, "Why bother? The problem is so huge, there is no way I can make a difference, so I might as well do nothing, and enjoy myself when I can." Let's do all we can to make those who say such things feel ever more unsure, and let's find numerous ways to make the experience so compelling that everyone wants to join the global quest for a war-free, inclusive, ecologically rich world.

Who Is William Tiller?

A Canadian, educated at the University of Toronto (BS, MS, PhD), Tiller was a physicist at the Westinghouse Research Laboratory for nine years and a professor at Stanford University's Department of Materials Science for thirty-four years. For thirty of those years, Tiller pursued the study of psychoenergetic science (expanding traditional science to include human consciousness). He has published over two hundred fifty traditional science papers, plus three technical books, and over 125 psychoenergetic science papers, as well as four books. He is now a professor emeritus at Stanford University in California, and continues his psychoenergetic science research in Arizona. www.tiller.org

WILLIAM
TILLER

My working hypothesis is that we humans are all spirits having a physical experience as we ride "The River of Life" together. Our spiritual parents dressed us in these biobodysuits and put us in this playpen that we call a universe in order to grow in coherence, in order to develop our gifts of intentionality, and in order to ultimately become what we were intended to become—effective cocreators with our spiritual parents! Sustained, consciously directed intention to manifest our highest ideals most readily allows us to materialize this goal. The practice of going within via daily meditation has most significantly helped to shape my life.

Who Is Justine Willis Toms?

Justine Willis Toms is the cofounder and managing producer of New Dimensions Media/World Broadcasting Network and New Dimensions Radio, a nonprofit, educational organization whose primary work is the production and distribution of the *New Dimensions* radio series heard worldwide. The network is a vortex for launching new trends, revealing timeless wisdom, and pushing the boundaries of form, language, and spirit. Founded in 1973 by Justine and her husband, Michael, it is a powerful and transformative archive with leading-edge thinkers, spiritual leaders, change agents, indigenous voices, artists, scientists, healers, ecologists, and social architects. This archive is now housed at Stanford University. For over three decades, Michael and Justine have been reporting on the history of the future. Justine has cohosted and produced countless radio shows, and she's the coauthor with Michael of *True Work: Doing What You Love and Loving What You Do* and author of *Small Pleasures: Finding Grace in a Chaotic World.* www.justinewillistoms.com, www.newdimensions.org

INSPIRATIONAL BOOKS THAT JUSTINE RECOMMENDS:

Earth-Based Psychology, Arnold Mindell

Sermon on the Mount According to Vedanta, Swami Prabhavananda

Letters of E. B. White, revised by E. B. White

The Red Tent, Anita Diamant

Refuge, Terry Tempest Williams

Call to Compassion, Aura Glaser

JUSTINE
WILLIS
TOMS

Notice what you are naturally enthusiastic about. Notice when your heart leaps up in joyous exuberance; notice when you are so excited about what you are doing that time seems to disappear. In these moments the voice of your spirit is speaking directly to you. By doing more of the things that bring you joy, you'll be tapping in to the unlimited power of the universe and all its creative abundance.

Who Is Michael Toms?

The cofounder, CEO and president, executive producer, and host of *New Dimensions Radio*, an internationally syndicated radio series, Michael Toms has been engaging in dialogue with the world's leading-edge thinkers, social architects, creative artists, scientists, and spiritual teachers, including such luminaries as Joseph Campbell, Buckminster Fuller, David Bohm, Alice Walker, H. H. the Dalai Lama, J. Krishnamurti, Maya Angelou, and many others. He served as executive producer and host of the award-winning *Deep Ecology for the 21st Century*, and his nationally acclaimed book *An Open Life: Joseph Campbell in Conversation with Michael Toms* has sold more than two hundred thousand copies. Seventeen additional books based on his interviews have been published, including *The Well of Creativity*, *The Soul of Business*, *The Power of Meditation and Prayer*, *Buddhism in the West*, and *At the Leading Edge*. More than one million of his diverse dialogues have been sold to individual listeners on cassette and CD throughout the world. He is the coauthor with his partner, Justine Willis Toms, of *True Work: Doing What You Love and Loving What You Do* and is the author of the bestselling *A Time for Choices: Deep Dialogues for Deep Democracy*. www.newdimensions.org

BOOKS THAT HAVE GREATLY INSPIRED MICHAEL'S LIFE:
The Life of Samuel Johnson, James Boswell
The Pleasures of Philosophy, Will Durant
The Essential Merton, Patrick J. Johnson
The Creative Process, Brewster Ghiselin
The Tibetan Book of Living and Dying, Sogyal Rinpoche

MICHAEL
TOMS

Hope is believing in spite of the evidence, and moving actively to change the evidence.

Who Is Lynne Twist?

Lynne Twist is the founder of the Soul of Money Institute, and the cofounder of the Hunger Project and the Pachamama Alliance. She is a global activist, fundraiser, and speaker who has raised hundreds of millions of dollars and trained thousands of fundraisers to be more effective in their work for organizations that serve the best instincts in us all—ending hunger, empowering women, nurturing children and youth, and contributing to the creation of a worldview of equality and sustainability for all life. She is the author of the book *The Soul of Money: Transforming Your Relationship with Money and Life.* Twist was named a Woman of Distinction at the United Nations by the International Health Awareness Network for her work to end hunger. www.soulofmoney.org

FIVE BOOKS THAT HAVE DEEPLY IMPACTED LYNNE'S LIFE JOURNEY:
Ishmael, Daniel Quinn
The Compassionate Universe, Eknath Easwaran
Gandhi the Man, Eknath Easwaran
Left to Tell, Immaculée Ilibagiza
Nectar in a Sieve, Kamala Markandaya

LYNNE
TWIST

The tide is turning deep in the human condition. In every culture, country, hamlet, and language, people are generating millions of projects, programs, and initiatives born of a yearning for an unprecedented transformation. We are collectively bringing forth an environmentally sustainable, spiritually fulfilling, and socially just human presence on this planet.

In nature, the forces that turn the tide come from high above and from the movement of the tide itself, a perfect metaphor for our time. We are the turning tide, each of us and all of us together, moved by the gravitational pull of our highest commitments and the profound power of collaboration.

Who Is Nina Utne?

Nina Rothschild Utne is the former CEO and current editor at large of *Utne Reader*, which she recently sold to Ogden Publications. Nina is a speaker on a wide range of topics that include motherhood as a training ground for business, the power of media to transform culture, spirituality and business, and the voice of independent media. She holds a BA in English and American literature from Harvard University and a master's degree in human development from St. Mary's University. Nina is also a founding member of the Headwaters Fund, City of Lakes Waldorf School, UnReasonable Women for the Earth, and Code Pink. www.utne.com

BOOKS THAT HAVE INSPIRED NINA:
Auntie Mame, Patrick Dennis
A number of essays by Ralph Waldo Emerson
If You Want to Write, Brenda Ueland
Refuge, Terry Tempest Williams
Tao Te Ching, Lao Tzu

NINA
UTNE

Advice to myself (and anyone else who could use it): Live fearlessly, love recklessly, and laugh as much as possible. Keep making new and improved mistakes. Don't be afraid to look foolish. When in doubt, keep quiet. Or not.

Who Is Evelyn Elsaesser-Valarino?

A worldwide authority in the field, Evelyn has studied Near-Death Experiences (NDEs) for over 25 years. She also investigates and researches Nearing-Death Awareness (specifically death-bed visions) and direct and spontaneous After-Death Communications. As well as writing about these extraordinary experiences around death, she also gives lectures and workshops and has participated in numerous TV documentaries and conferences across Europe and the USA. She's a member of the board of directors of the French Institute for Research on Extraordinary Experiences (INREES) in Paris and is the European coordinator of IANDS (International Association for Near-Death Studies). Her many published books include *Clinical Handbook of Extraordinary Experiences,* her novel *Talking with Angel,* and *Lessons from the Light* with Kenneth Ring. www.elsaesser-valarino.com

FAVORITE BOOKS OF EVELYN'S:

Heading Toward Omega, Kenneth Ring
On Children and Death, Elisabeth Kübler-Ross
Children of the Light, Cherie Sutherland
The Private Worlds of Dying Children, Myra Bluebond-Langner
Love Lives On, Louis LaGrand

EVELYN
ELSAESSER-
VALARINO

Rossiter Worthington Raymond wrote a long time ago, "For life is eternal and love is immortal and death is only a horizon, and a horizon is nothing save the limit of our sight."

The time has come for us to get closer to this horizon and populate a new land, in which many have glanced at a dimension being revealed with urgency these last decades. I name this the land of near-death experiences, nearing death awareness, after-death communications and other spiritual experiences. These are normal human experiences happening to ordinary individuals and taking them on a path of transformation, unfettering them from the fear of death. The deeper and more often we penetrate into this land, the better we will glimpse beyond the known limit and reinforce our conviction that hope is indeed located beyond the horizon.

Who Is Sarah van Gelder?

Sarah Ruth van Gelder is the cofounder and executive editor of *Yes!* magazine and a board member of its nonprofit publisher, Positive Futures Network. Since its inception in 1996, Sarah has edited issues of *Yes!* while also writing and speaking on leading-edge innovations that show that another world is not only possible, but is being created. Topics include alternatives to prisons, sustainable food and agriculture, nonviolence and active peacemaking, corporate power, liberated culture, and life-sustaining economics. Sarah lives on the Port Madison Reservation, home of Chief Seattle, where she serves on the board of trustees of the Suquamish Foundation, a tribally chartered foundation supporting the resurgence of native culture. She has lived and worked in China, India, and South America; is raising two young adult children; and was a founding member of Winslow Cohousing, one of the first U.S. cohousing communities. www.yesmagazine.org

BOOKS THAT HAVE MOST INFLUENCED SARAH:

Earth Democracy, Vandana Shiva
Strategy for a Living Revolution, George Lakey
Grassroots Post-Modernism, Gustavo Esteva and Madhu Suri Prakash
Utopian Legacies, John Mohawk
Revolution and Evolution in the Twentieth Century,
    Grace Lee Boggs and Jimmy Boggs

SARAH VAN **GELDER**

We live at the most dangerous time in recorded history. Big corporations, big finance, big media, big military, big technology (at least some of them)—well meaning or not—are destroying our living systems. We need to relearn the soul-satisfying ways of communities—urban and rural—living in harmony with local ecosystems, and we have to recognize what every spiritual and humanist tradition teaches: life is what is important—not money—and every single human being is precious and has rights. Fortunately, all over the world, people are creating green, diverse, equitable ways to live together, make livelihoods, and resolve conflicts. Together, these efforts are our best hope.

Who Is Max Velmans?

Originally an electrical engineer, then a psychologist and philosopher, Max developed his courses on consciousness over a period of thirty years at the University of London, where they were amongst the first to reintroduce the study of consciousness into modern psychology. He has been involved in many initiatives to foster the development of consciousness studies, including the foundation of the Consciousness and Experiential Psychology Section of the British Psychological Society, which he chaired from 2003 to 2006. His work focuses mainly on the deeper theoretical problems of consciousness, viewed from both Western and Eastern perspectives, and he has over one hundred publications on this subject, including his widely acclaimed book *Understanding Consciousness*. He has given numerous international keynotes, seminars, and invited lectures in this area. www.goldsmiths.ac.uk/psychology/staff/velmans.php

FIVE BOOKS THAT HAVE INFLUENCED MAX:

The Doors of Perception, Aldous Huxley
Memories, Dreams, Reflections, Carl Jung
On the Taboo Against Knowing Who You Are, Alan Watts
Man, God, and the Universe, I. K. Taimni
Sceptical Essays, Bertrand Russell

MAX VELMANS

The existence of consciousness is often thought to be the greatest mystery in science, while the existence of matter is taken for granted. But the existence of matter is equally mysterious. Why should there be anything rather than nothing? Nor are there good reasons to believe that consciousness emerged from matter. Rather, consciousness and matter co-emerged and continue to co-evolve from the primal event in which our universe was born. Far from being strangers in a strange land, human life and consciousness are natural expressions of the universe in ways that we are only beginning to understand. We are embodied and embedded in a mystery—and, in the depths of our being, we *are* that mystery.

Who Is Mathis Wackernagel?

Mathis Wackernagel, PhD, created, with Professor William Rees, the ecological footprint—a now widely used tool for measuring sustainability. Wackernagel is a founder and executive director of Global Footprint Network, a charitable research organization based in California, which is working to create a sustainable economy by advancing the use of ecological footprints. Mathis has advised governments, companies, and civil society organizations on the possibility of living well within the limits of one planet. His awards include a 2007 Skoll Award for Social Entrepreneurship, a 2006 World Wildlife Fund (WWF) Award for Conservation Merit, and the 2005 Herman Daly Award from the U.S. Society for Ecological Economics. www.footprintnetwork.org

FIVE BOOKS THAT HAVE INSPIRED MATHIS:

For the Common Good, Herman E. Daly

The Limits to Growth, Donella H. Meadows, Dennis L. Meadows, Jørgen Randers, and William W. Behrens III

Henry Hikes to Fitchburg, Donald B. Johnson

Man's Search for Meaning, Viktor Frankl

To Have or To Be?, Erich Fromm

MATHIS
WACKERNAGEL

It has become clear that humanity is consuming resources and exploiting ecosystems at a rate the planet cannot sustain. But mankind's greatest challenge for the twenty-first century—to live within our ecological means—is also our greatest opportunity. In the past, we've addressed limited resources by brutality and by leaving large segments of humanity in the dust. Once we recognize resource constraints and deal with them in a rational way, we can have a relatively stable, peaceful coexistence. Learning to live within the means of one Earth is a battle that will require the best in human spirit and engineering. And we all must win, or everyone will lose.

Who Is Brenda Wade?

Recognized as one of the most renowned psychologists in America, Dr. Brenda Wade is best known for her dynamic, love-centered approach to transformation. She has earned numerous awards as a psychologist, author, television host, producer, keynote speaker, and seminar leader. She hosted the nationally syndicated *Can this Marriage Be Saved?* and appeared on shows such as the *Today* show and *Oprah*. In San Francisco, she hosts *Black Renaissance*. Dr. Wade authored *Power Choices: 7 Signposts on Your Journey to Wholeness, Love, Joy, and Peace*, and both produced and hosted the national PBS special *Power Choices*. Dr. Wade also authored *Love Lessons* and *What Mama Couldn't Tell Us about Love*. www.docwade.com

FIVE OF BRENDA'S FAVORITE BOOKS:

H. P. B., Sylvia Cranston
I Know Why the Caged Bird Sings, Maya Angelou
What Mama Couldn't Tell Us About Love, Dr. Brenda Wade
Autobiography of a Yogi, Paramahansa Yogananda
The Luminous Darkness, Dr. Howard Thurman

BRENDA
WADE

As every heart heals and can fully open to love (human and divine), there will be love in every home, in every community, then love in every nation—this is the key to peace in the world. My vision and my mission include seeking to express the divine in every thought, word, and action. To know ourselves as divine allows us to recognize the divine in others. This truth, which underlies every faith, uplifts and unites all beings. Repeat this decree often: I am one with life, and the peace of life radiates through my every thought, word, and action.

Who Is Razeena Wagiet?

Dr. Razeena Wagiet is a South African active in advancing environment and education work. She holds academic and professional qualifications in natural and social sciences, and she has a PhD in environmental education. As environment adviser to the previous national minister, Razeena was key in establishing the National Environmental Education Programme, which introduced and pioneered environmental studies into the national curriculum. She is currently the executive director for People and Conservation in South African National Parks. Razeena also contributes widely to furthering environmental sustainability and awareness by participating on decision-making boards and advisory structures. One such position is the cochair she holds for the Earth Charter International Council. www.sanparks.org, www.earthcharter.org

FIVE BOOKS THAT HAVE SIGNIFICANTLY SHAPED RAZEENA'S LIFE:

Conversations with God (Books 1, 2 & 3), by Neale Donald Walsch
The Camino, Shirley MacLaine
The Power of Now, Eckhart Tolle
The Alchemist, Paulo Coelho
Long Walk to Freedom, Nelson Mandela

RAZEENA
WAGIET

I envisage . . . a peaceful world where we live and interact as a united people; liberated from the divisive confines of nationalism, racism, and religious sectarianism; cocreating an equitable and just society that coexists in harmony with nature and our surroundings.

I visualize. . . a wonderful world. A manifested universal spirituality; omnipresent love, compassion, and respect; a healthy, ecological, sustainable planet.

Who Is Alice Walker?

Alice Walker is one of the most prolific and important writers of our time, known for her literary fiction, including the Pulitzer Prize–winning *The Color Purple* (now a major Broadway play), her many volumes of poetry, and her powerful nonfiction collections. Ms. Walker has also published several children's books: *There Is a Flower at the Tip of My Nose Smelling Me* is her most recent work for children and adults. In the fall of 2006 she published a book of spiritual ruminations with a progressive political edge: *We Are the Ones We Have Been Waiting For: Inner Light in a Time of Darkness.*

FIVE BOOKS THAT HAVE INFLUENCED ALICE GREATLY:

The Prophet, Kahlil Gibran

Pride and Prejudice, Jane Austen

Raja-Yoga, Swami Vivekananda

The Secret Doctrine, Helena Petrovna Blavatsky

Heart, The Agni Yoga Society

ALICE WALKER

Most countries in the world need to choose different parents, and these parents exist. They are the father and mother who did not ravage, rape, and plunder; the father and mother who did not exterminate and sell and buy into slavery. The father and mother who did not seek domination over the Earth.

I imagine these parents sitting quietly on a hillside waiting for us to notice that a big problem humans face is that we do not know our own founding mothers; we do not know our own founding fathers.

We think we are orphans. And have no flag.

Who Is B. Alan Wallace?

B. Alan Wallace, PhD, has taught Buddhist meditation since 1976. Having devoted fourteen years to training as a Tibetan Buddhist monk, ordained by H. H. the Dalai Lama, he went on to earn an undergraduate degree in physics and the philosophy of science at Amherst College and a doctorate in religious studies at Stanford University. He brings unique experience and skills to the challenge of seeking ways to integrate Buddhist contemplative practices and Western science to advance the study of the mind. He is the founder and president of the Santa Barbara Institute for Consciousness Studies. www.sbinstitute.com

B. ALAN
WALLACE

For tens of thousands of years the human race gradually biologically evolved in response to a gradually changing environment. During that time we sought our happiness and well-being largely by looking outward to an abundant planet on which we have hunted and foraged for the necessities and pleasures of life. But over the past few centuries, the ecosphere has undergone many dramatic shifts resulting from a rapidly expanding human population empowered by the knowledge and might of science and technology. With each year the rate of change increases, making it impossible for biological evolution to keep pace and ensure our survival and procreation. For the flourishing of humanity and our very survival as a species, the time has now come for us to evolve spiritually, not biologically. Nature demands that we shift our emphasis from outer pleasures and gratification to the quest for inner well-being through the cultivation of the human mind, heart, and spirit. The time to tap the deepest potentials of human consciousness is at hand, as we embark on the greatest adventure in the history of our species.

Who Is Stewart Wallis?

Stewart Wallis graduated in Natural Sciences from Cambridge University and then obtained a master's degree in business and economics at London Business School. He began his career in sales and marketing before joining the World Bank in Washington, D.C., where he worked on industrial and financial development in East Asia, and becoming administrator of the Young Professionals Programme. He went on to work for Robinson Packaging, where he became the managing director and led a successful business turnaround. He joined Oxfam in 1992 as the international director, with responsibility, latterly, for twenty-five hundred staff in seventy countries and for all Oxfam's policy, research, development, and emergency work worldwide. He was awarded the OBE for services to Oxfam in 2002 and, a year later, joined the New Economics Foundation in London as executive director. Stewart's other focused areas include global governance, the future of capitalism, and the moral economy. He lives in the UK, is a passionate landscape photographer, and has five children. www.neweconomics.org

FIVE OF STEWART'S FAVORITE BOOKS:

Small Is Beautiful, E. F. Schumacher
Mountain Light, Galen Rowell
The Poisonwood Bible, Barbara Kingsolver
Northern Lights, Phillip Pullman
The Road Less Travelled, M. Scott Peck

STEWART
WALLIS

We are at a Galileo/Copernicus moment in history. We need to radically rethink our economic system and move rapidly to build a "moral economy." Currently we are "running faster and faster," at possibly terminal costs to ourselves and our planet. Yet we don't make ourselves any happier, nor do we solve the problems of global poverty and inequality. My vision is a "moral economy" which promotes the growth of collective and individual well-being rather than growth in GDP, ensures every human being on the planet has their social and economic rights met, and does so in a way that leaves a healthier and more sustainable planet for our children and grandchildren and for all forms of life.

Who Is Neale Donald Walsch?

Neale Donald Walsch is the author of twenty-four books, including six *New York Times* bestsellers. Books in his nine-volume *Conversations with God* series have sold over 7.5 million copies and have been translated into thirty-seven languages. Among his other titles are *Friendship with God, Communion with God, What God Wants, Tomorrow's God, Home with God: In a Life that Never Ends,* and *Happier than God.* He travels the globe offering workshops, retreats, and seminars helping people to integrate the revolutionary spiritual principles of Conversations with God into their daily lives. www.nealedonaldwalsch.com

BOOKS THAT HAVE TOUCHED NEALE'S LIFE IN A POWERFUL WAY:

Stranger in a Strange Land, Robert Heinlein

Handbook to Higher Consciousness, Ken Keyes

Be Here Now, Ram Dass

Emergence, Barbara Marx Hubbard

Loving What Is, Byron Katie

Jump Time, Jean Houston

NEALE
DONALD
WALSCH

I see humanity rewriting its Cultural Story. This is happening right now. The shift is away from the central idea of Separation to a new idea embracing the unity of all things. This includes the Oneness of That Which Is Divine with all that is. When this shift is complete (and our opportunity is to make it so), all the world will change, killing and oppression will disappear, no one will ever again deliberately hurt another, and we will get on with our true purpose in life: to evolve the human spirit through the expression and experiencing of our Divinity.

Who Is Stephanie Walshe?

Stephanie Walshe is the founder of Child Star Planners, established in 1999. Her biggest inspiration to discover astrology was her youngest son, who was a very challenging four-year-old at the time! It opened her mind completely and made her realize how we all just scratch the surface when it comes to understanding who we are and why we do the things we do. Through the use of astrology, Stephanie is able to identify key aspects of a child's nature, needs, and talents, from which she produces custom books designed to help parents understand each of their children in a wholly constructive and pragmatic way. Called the Super Nanny of Astrology by her clients, Stephanie has written several hundred individual books for parents of children from all around the world and takes a personal delight in hearing from the many families who have found Child Star Planners a major help in their children's upbringing. www.childstarplanners.com

WORKS THAT HAVE INFLUENCED AND INSPIRED STEPHANIE:

The Prophet and other writings, Kahlil Gibran

Einstein's Beetle, Mark Southworth

Turner in his Time, Andrew Wilton

Great Expectations, Charles Dickens

Anna Karenina, Leo Tolstoy

"The Pylons" and other works by the poet Stephen Spender

STEPHANIE
WALSHE

Every child who comes into this world has hopes, needs, and aspirations, no matter what environment they have been born into. Their dreams need to be cherished, their needs understood. What better gift can parents give than to assist each of their children to shine brightly and to help them achieve their most heartfelt dreams? It is within our power to do so if we choose, and in so doing to carve out a brighter, more harmonious future for all generations to come.

Who Is C. Jean Weidemann?

Celia Jean Weidemann, PhD, is considered a pioneer in integrating gender issues into mainstream international economic development and microfinance. For the past thirty-five years she has worked toward more equitable access to the world's resources in thirty countries on five continents. She has held positions with the United Nations, World Bank, U.S. Congress, and State Department/USAID, and numerous universities, private firms, and foreign governments. She has authored more than forty books and publications, and has helped found two global women's organizations with thirty thousand members. She founded and is president of the Weidemann Foundation. www.createglobalchange.org

FIVE INFLUENTIAL BOOK/SONGS IN JEAN'S LIFE:
Seven Years in Tibet, Heinrich Harrer
Man's Search for Meaning, Viktor Frankl
The Handmaid's Tale, Margaret Atwood
The Poisonwood Bible, Barbara Kingsolver
"All You Need Is Love," The Beatles

C. JEAN
WEIDEMANN

Each of us can create global change if we choose to look at the world's current *challenges* as *opportunities* to live from a place of interconnectedness—to others and to this fragile planet. If we meld the spiritual parts of our beings with heart-centered activism, we *can* create social and economic equality, access to resources, and peace. In these trying times, we can transform ourselves, our communities, and the world—from preschoolers saving pennies for books for their counterparts on other continents, to senior citizens volunteering in local soup kitchens, to villagers replanting forests or making bricks for their new schools.

Who Is Tony Whitbread?

Tony has been working for the Sussex Wildlife Trust for twenty years, becoming chief executive in 2006. Before that he worked in the Chief Scientist Team of the then Nature Conservancy Council. He has contributed to numerous committees, initiatives, and programs at local, regional, and national levels influencing planning and policy matters. Tony has been instrumental in particular in promoting large-scale approaches to nature conservation. This philosophy has surfaced in documents such as the Sussex Wildlife Trust's Vision for the Wildlife of Sussex, and in national initiatives such as the Wildlife Trust's Living Landscape theme. Increasingly, links have been made with large-scale approaches in Europe such as the Pan European Ecological Network and the European Wildland Initiative, all aiming to shift nature conservation from a preservationist approach to one that promotes the rebuilding of ecologically rich, functional ecosystems.

FIVE BOOKS THAT INFLUENCED TONY THE MOST:
"Blueprint for Survival," The Ecologist
Collapse, Jared Diamond
Where the Wild Things Were, William Stolzenburg
Grazing Ecology and Forest History, Frans Vera
Peak Everything, Richard Heinberg

TONY
WHITBREAD

This is the best time to be alive! The world is about to change from one that sees biodiversity—nature—as an unimportant externality to be exploited, to one that recognizes its central role in our survival. We will develop living landscapes and living seas throughout the globe where nature is enhanced, expanded, and interlinked, making functional ecosystems that support us and wildlife. This will drive, and be driven by, cultural change. There may be less "stuff," but lives will be richer, in harmony with nature, and sustainable. And we have the privilege to live through the change. Living Landscape, Living Seas, Living Lightly.

Who Is John Whitmore?

A privileged, but wartime, childhood drove John to become a professional racing driver to challenge and find himself. After a British and European Championship and subsequent experience in business, John embarked on a psycho–spiritual search in California and elsewhere to find his real purpose in life—which he knew lay beyond money and success. John became deeply engaged in many aspects of social change and political activism, from the United States to the Soviet Union, and from Nicaragua to Israel. He also made a psychological film, ran ski and tennis schools based on the Inner Game, became a business consultant, and wrote five books, of which the most popular is *Coaching for Performance*, now published in twenty languages. John writes articles, including an environmental column for a British national newspaper, and was cofounder of several pioneering conferences, the most recent being the annual Be the Change event in London. He is now the chair of Performance Consultants International—a global consultancy in leadership, sustainability, transformation, and learning and development—and of the Institute of Human Excellence in Australia. He loves to ski, when not trying to change the world! www.bethechange.org.uk, www.performanceconsultants.com, www.ihexcellence.org

BOOKS THAT HAVE INSPIRED JOHN GREATLY:
The Greening of America, Charles Reich
Supernature, Lyall Watson
The Inner Game of Tennis, Timothy Gallwey
Confessions of an Economic Hitman, John Perkins
A New Earth, Eckhart Tolle

JOHN
WHITMORE

Despite the depressing news that besieges us, I am humbled to be alive at this extraordinary moment in human history. For the first time we have the opportunity to meet the needs of everyone on Earth, and for the first time, too, we have the capacity to destroy all life. We face the ultimate choice between cooperation or devastation, resignation or responsibility. We are at the tipping point of conscious evolution. I remain fiercely optimistic. We are neither the physical nor the intelligent center of the universe; however, our only limits are our own self-limiting beliefs. Let's release ourselves now.

Who Is Dennis Whittle?

Dennis Whittle is the CEO and cofounder of GlobalGiving, the world's leading marketplace for philanthropy and aid projects. GlobalGiving allows donors and community-based projects to connect directly, enabling donors to see exactly what their money is used for, and enabling project leaders anywhere to talk directly to their supporters. Through the GlobalGiving marketplace, over sixteen hundred projects in one hundred countries have raised over twenty million dollars from fifty thousand individual donors and some of the world's most innovative and socially committed companies as of 2009. Prior to GlobalGiving, Dennis worked for fourteen years at the World Bank in countries such as Niger, Indonesia, and Russia. In the late 1990s, he was asked to lead the World Bank's innovation efforts, and he and his team created the Development Marketplace, an open-access competition where anyone in the world can compete for funding. Dennis has a degree in religious studies from the University of North Carolina, Chapel Hill, where he was a Morehead Scholar, and a master's degree in public policy from the Woodrow Wilson School.

BOOKS THAT HAVE INFLUENCED DENNIS:

Surely You're Joking, Mr. Feynman, Richard Feynman, Ralph Leighton, et al.
The Selfish Gene, Richard Dawkins
The Hedgehog and the Fox, Isaiah Berlin
Ubiquity: Why Catastrophes Happen, Mark Buchanan
*The Monk and the Riddle: The Art of Creating a Life
    While Making a Living,* Randy Komisar
My Past and Thoughts, Alexander Herzen

DENNIS
WHITTLE

Dream it and you can do it—sometimes. Optimism with sober expectations is the key to happiness and, maybe, success. Work hard and try to follow your dreams, but realize that randomness in life often trumps all, so don't be too hard on yourself if you don't succeed. If you are fabulously successful, be modest, and realize that luck played a big role (in addition to your hard work, vision, charm, and good looks). Avoid putting all your eggs in one basket—maximize your chances for success and transformation by doing lots of experiments and ventures over time.

Who Is Terrie M. Williams?

Terrie Williams wanted to save the world. This thinking lies at the very core of who she is and is reflected in her work and community service. In 1988 she started the Terrie Williams Agency, handling big-ticket entertainment, sports, business, and Fortune 500 names. Profits from her business enabled her to kick-start several philanthropic projects, including The Stay Strong Foundation. She is the acclaimed author of several books, including *Stay Strong: Simple Life Lessons for Teens* and *The Personal Touch: What You Really Need to Succeed in Today's Fast-Paced Business World.* She is an inspirational speaker and one of her latest books, *Black Pain: It Just Looks Like We're Not Hurting,* highlights the untold story of depression amongst African-Americans. www.terriewilliams.com

BOOKS THAT INSPIRED TERRIE:
The Highly Sensitive Person, Elaine Aron
Make Your Creative Dreams Real, Sark
One Day My Soul Just Opened Up: 40 Days and Nights Toward Spiritual Strength and Personal Growth, Iyanla Vanzant
The Freedom Writers Diary, The Freedom Writers and Erin Gruwell
In the Spirit, Susan Taylor

TERRIE M.
WILLIAMS

Dealing with people the way you really feel at any given moment—good, bad, or ugly—is not always an easy thing to do. Hiding and lying about unpleasant moods might seem like a way to avoid trouble, but it actually does more damage than simply being honest. The moment you stop pretending and playing a role from behind your mask, you open up the door, giving permission to others to follow suit. If we can get to the place where we show up as our genuine selves and let each other see who we really are, the awe-inspiring ripple effect will change the world.

Who Is Graham Wilson?

Graham Wilson is a pioneer in the field of natural health and personal growth. He brought together for the first time in the public arena a great variety of hitherto fragmented alternative ways of being.

He is the founder of the Mind Body Spirit festivals in England (1977–present), the United States (1982–1983), and Australia (1989–present). They have the largest attendances and are the longest running of any New Age expos. Their unique formula created a blueprint for future shows of this kind.

In 1980 Graham founded the London Natural Health Clinic, Europe's first holistic health center. In the 1990s he promoted Deepak Chopra, Wayne Dyer, John Gray, Neale Donald Walsch, and Denise Linn. grahamwilson@ihug.co.nz

BOOKS THAT HAVE GIVEN GUIDANCE AND INSPIRATION:
The Theory of Celestial Influence, Rodney Collin
Space, Time & Medicine, Larry Dossey, M.D.
Laws of Manifestation, David Spangler
Hug the Monster, David Miln Smith, PhD, and Sandra Leicester
Health Defence, Dr. Paul Clayton

GRAHAM
WILSON

I see mankind on the threshold of a transformation that will provide the impetus for us to extend ourselves beyond our self-imposed limitations toward our full potential. As we develop a greater awareness of our environment, our planet, and ourselves, we are recognizing the need for a shared commitment to enhance life in a lasting, practical way. A way that appreciates the beauty of nature, pure air and water, natural foods, and above all the inherent goodness and promise of all beings.

I see humanity gradually surrendering to the oneness of all things and recognizing the essential interrelatedness of mind, body, and spirit. It is a vision for the paradise of tomorrow for which we must struggle today.

Who Is David Woodward?

David Woodward is an independent consultant on development issues and author of *Debt, Adjustment and Poverty in Developing Countries, The Next Crisis? Direct and Equity Investment in Developing Countries,* and *Growth Isn't Working.* His main areas of work are the integration of development and environmental agendas, elaborating an alternative paradigm of economic development, the democratization of global economic governance, globalization, and health.

David has previously worked as an economic adviser in the Foreign and Commonwealth Office, as a technical assistant to the UK executive director to the IMF and World Bank, as a development economist in the Strategy Unit of the World Health Organization, as an economic policy adviser to Save the Children (UK), and as head of the New Global Economy program at the New Economics Foundation (NEF). www.neweconomics.org

DAVID
WOODWARD

Humanity faces two profound challenges. Poverty eradication is a moral imperative; stopping global warming is a practical necessity for our survival. We can only meet these challenges together—yet our current model of development makes poverty reduction dependent on ever-increasing overconsumption among the rich. We are thus forced to choose between morality and necessity, and prevented from achieving either goal. We must rethink the whole basis of the global economy, to make it the servant, not the master, of the world's people. And this means applying in international institutions democratic principles taken for granted at the national level—transparency, accountability, and equality of representation for all.

Who Is Lily Yeh?

Lily Yeh is an internationally celebrated artist and activist who brings the transformative power of art to the most impoverished communities in the world through participatory and multifaceted projects that foster community empowerment, improve physical environments, promote economic development, and preserve indigenous art and culture. Her work at the Village of Arts and Humanities in inner-city North Philadelphia from 1986 to 2004 has won her the reputation as one of America's most innovative grassroots urban designers and social pioneers. She was honored with the 2001 Rudy Bruner Gold Award for Urban Excellence and the Ford Foundation's 2003 Leadership for the Changing World Award.

Her current work with the children of migrant workers in China and genocide survivors in west Rwanda, under the auspices of Barefoot Artists, Inc., the nonprofit organization she founded in 2002, aims to bring healing, self-empowerment, and social change through innovative art, educational, and entreprenurial initiatives. Her work in designing and building the Rugerero Genocide Memorial in Rwanda brought dignity and beauty to the survivors.

When people see beauty, they see hope.

BOOKS THAT HAVE DEEPLY INSPIRED LILY'S LIFE PATH:

Tao Te Ching, Lao Tzu
An Autobiography, Mahatma Gandhi
Letters to a Young Poet, Rainer Maria Rilke
The Mythic Image, Joseph Campbell
The Tao of Physics, Fritjof Capra

LILY
YEH

Beauty is the spark that lights up the night sky. To create beauty in places of great suffering restores human dignity and brings hope and joy. Any action from the heart is a beautiful act. It brings healing through our act of serving. It reconnects us to the life force that sets the sun, moon, and stars in motion in the sky.

We are born with the flame of light within us. Get in touch with that light so we become empowered to walk our paths in light and love. When fear sets in, embrace it with courage. Then magic and transformation happen.

The Earth Is Precious

In 1854, the "Great White Chief" in Washington made an offer for a large area of Indian land and promised a "reservation" for the Indian people. The tribal leader, Chief Seattle, replied to Washington with a statement which is now widely regarded as one of the most beautiful and profound statements on the environment ever made. Here is that inspirational reply:

How can you buy or sell the sky, the warmth of the land? The idea is strange to us.

If we do not own the freshness of the air and the sparkle of the water, how can you buy them?

Every part of this earth is sacred to my people.

Every shining pine needle, every sand shore, every mist in the dark woods, every clearing and humming insect is holy in the memory and experience of my people. The sap which courses through the trees carries the memories of the red man.

The white man's dead forget the country of their birth when they go to walk among the stars. Our dead never forget this beautiful earth, for it is the mother of the red man.

We are part of the earth and it is part of us.

The perfumed flowers are our sisters; the deer, the horse, the great eagle, these are our brothers.

The rocky crests, the juices in the meadows, the body heat of the pony, and man all belong to the same family.

So when the Great Chief in Washington sends word that he wishes to buy our land, he asks much of us. So, the Great Chief sends word he will reserve us a place so that we can live comfortably to ourselves.

He will be our father and we will be his children. So we will consider your offer to buy our land.

But it will not be easy. For this land is sacred to us.

The shining water in the streams and rivers is not just water but the blood of our ancestors.

If we sell you land, you must remember that it is sacred, and you must teach your children that it is sacred, and that each ghostly reflection in the clear water of the lakes tells of events and memories in the life of my people.

The water's murmur is the voice of my father's father.

The rivers are our brothers, they quench our thirst. The rivers carry our canoes, and feed our children. If we sell you our land, you must remember, and teach your children, that the rivers are our brothers, and yours, and you must henceforth give the rivers the kindness you would give any brother....

We know that the white man does not understand our ways. One portion of land is the same to him as the next, for he is a stranger who comes in the night and takes from the land whatever he needs.

The earth is not his brother, but his enemy, and when he has conquered it, he moves on.

He leaves his fathers' graves behind, and he does not care. He kidnaps the earth from his children, and he does not care.

His fathers' graves and his children's birthright are forgotten. He treats his mother, the earth, and his brother, the sky, as things to be bought, plundered, sold like sheep or bright beads.

His appetite will devour the earth and leave behind only a desert.

I do not know. Our ways are different from your ways.

The sight of your cities pains the eye of the red man. But perhaps it is because the red man is a savage and does not understand.

There is no quiet place in the white man's cities. No place to hear the unfurling of leaves in spring or the rustle of insects' wings.

But perhaps it is because I am a savage and do not understand.

The clatter only seems to insult the ears. And what is there to life if a man cannot hear the lonely cry of a whippoorwill or the arguments of the frogs around a pond at night? I am a red man and do not understand.

The Indian prefers the soft sound of the wind darting over the face of a pond, and the smell of the wind itself, cleaned by a midday rain, or scented with the piñon pine.

The air is precious to the red man, for all things share the same breath—the beast, the tree, the man, they all share the same breath.

The white man does not seem to notice the air he breathes. Like a man dying for many days, he is numb to the stench.

But if we sell you our land, you must remember that the air is precious to us, that the air shares its spirit with all life it supports. The wind that gave our grandfather his first breath also receives his last sigh. And the wind must also give our children the spirit of life.

And if we sell you our land, you must keep it apart and sacred, as a place where even the white man can go to taste the wind that is sweetened by the meadow's flowers.

So we will consider your offer to buy our land. If we decide to accept, I will make one condition: The white man must treat the beasts of this land as his brothers.

I am a savage and I do not understand any other way.

I have seen a thousand rotting buffaloes on the prairie, left by the white man who shot them from a passing train.

I am a savage and I do not understand how the smoking iron horse can be more important than the buffalo that we kill only to stay alive.

What is man without the beasts? If all the beasts were gone, men would die from a great loneliness of spirit.

For whatever happens to the beasts, soon happens to man. All things are connected.

You must teach your children that the ground beneath their feet is the ashes of our grandfathers. So that they will respect the land, tell your children that the earth is rich with the lives of our kin.

Teach your children what we have taught our children, that the earth is our mother.

Whatever befalls the earth befalls the sons of the earth. If men spit upon the ground, they spit upon themselves.

This we know: The earth does not belong to man; man belongs to the earth. This we know.

All things are connected like the blood which unites one family. All things are connected.

Whatever befalls the earth befalls the sons of the earth. Man did not weave the web of life: he is merely a strand in it. Whatever he does to the web, he does to himself....

Even the white man, whose God walks and talks with him as friend to friend, cannot be exempt from the common destiny.

We may be brothers after all; we shall see.

One thing we know, which the white man may one day discover—our God is the same God.

You may think now that you own him as you wish to own our land; but you cannot. He is the God of man, and his compassion is equal for the red man and the white.

The earth is precious to him, and to harm the earth is to heap contempt on its Creator.

The white too shall pass; perhaps sooner than all other tribes. Continue to contaminate your bed, and you will one night suffocate in your own waste.

But in your perishing you will shine brightly, fired by the strength of the God who brought you to this land and for some special purpose gave you dominion over this land and over the red man.

That destiny is a mystery to us, for we do not understand when the buffalo are all slaughtered, the wild horses are tamed, the secret corners of the forest heavy with scent of many men, and the view of the ripe hills blotted by talking wires.

Where is the thicket? Gone.
Where is the eagle? Gone.
And what is it to say goodbye to the swift pony and the hunt?
The end of living and the beginning of survival.

Peace

By Eileen Caddy MBE (Findhorn Foundation, Scotland)
August 26, 1917–December 13, 2006

"Universal peace starts within each individual. It starts with me and you. As we think, so we are. As a nation of people thinks, so it is. Let's look within our hearts. Until we bring harmony into our everyday lives and learn to love the people around us, how can we hope to bring universal peace into the world? We cannot fight for peace. A person of peace does not resist war, but practices peace. As we make changes within ourselves, we will find that they have taken place in those around us as well. When we are at perfect peace within ourselves, all conflict will disappear and we will see humanity through the eyes of love. Where there is love there is peace."

Thank you to Liza Hollingshead, Eileen's official biographer, for selecting the above piece which was taken from a talk given in India many years ago. And thank you also to Eileen's son Jonathon, who granted us kind permission to access and publish her work.

For those not aware, Eileen Caddy was one of three founding members of the Findhorn Foundation in Scotland, UK, a spiritual community, eco-village, and an international center for holistic education, which is helping to unfold a new human consciousness and create a positive and sustainable future. Sadly, Eileen passed away in December 2006 at the age of eighty-nine.

From its early conception, Findhorn's vision was always to create a community that appreciated the connection between nature and humans. And its philosophy and teachings today are every bit as relevant as when the foundation first began in 1962. In fact, many would say, even more so.

www.findhorn.org

About the Author

William Murtha is a writer, philanthropist, and global activist for issues related to personal, social, and global transformation, the environment, and social responsibility. Several years after a life-changing near-death accident in 1999, he left behind everything that he'd ever worked hard to achieve to pursue his dream of becoming a writer. Selling his business and turning away from a stressful career in sales management, William finally answered the calling to write full-time so that he could bring his inspiring new ideas out into the open.

Having worked in construction and development management until 2005, William sold his shares in the business he had founded and instead began concentrating fully on writing and other creative projects. One of those initiatives, The Imagination Project, is a nonprofit organization set up solely to help those emerging young luminaries, writers, and filmmakers who are focusing their life's work on many of the most critical issues of our time. To fund and kick-start this exciting project, William managed to persuade over two hundred global leaders, change-makers, and visionaries, from across all sectors of change, to donate short written vision statements toward the book you are now reading.

Professionally, William is a member of several globally recognized organizations that are helping to raise awareness about some of the most critically important issues of our time, including Schumacher College, the Institute of Noetic Sciences, and the Scientific and Medical Network.

His first publication, *Dying for a Change*, which was released in September 2009, tells the gripping account of his terrifying near-death experience, when he was washed off a sea wall by a twenty-foot freak wave close to his home in England. Drowning, losing consciousness, and convinced his time was up, William experienced a one-in-a-billion miracle that went on to totally change his life.

He has three daughters; Jenna, Olivia, and Kitty, and lives in Devon, a county on the western coast of Britain.

www.williammurtha.com

To Our Readers

Conari Press, an imprint of Red Wheel/Weiser, publishes books on topics ranging from spirituality, personal growth, and relationships to women's issues, parenting, and social issues. Our mission is to publish quality books that will make a difference in people's lives—how we feel about ourselves, and how we relate to one another. We value integrity, compassion, and receptivity, both in the books we publish and in the way we do business.

Our readers are our most important resource, and we value your input, suggestions, and ideas about what you would like to see published. Please feel free to contact us, to request our latest book catalog, or to be added to our mailing list.

Conari Press
An imprint of Red Wheel/Weiser, LLC
500 Third Street, Suite 230
San Francisco, CA 94107
www.redwheelweiser.com